How to Get a Great English Degree: A Guide for Undergraduates

By Francis Gilbert

Francis Gilbert

This edition first published in 2013 by FGI publishing, London
www.francisgilbert.co.uk

ISBN-10: 1492282189
ISBN-13: 978-1492282181

CONTENTS

DEDICATION

To all the lecturers & undergraduates I have taught and have supported me in my teaching.

ACKNOWLEDGMENTS

First, huge thanks must go to my wife, Erica Wagner, for always supporting me with my writing and teaching. Second, I'm very grateful to all the students and teachers who have helped me write this book, espccially Jane Desmarais, M. Griffiths & Mary-Claire Halvorson. Any mistakes in the book are entirely mine and they have no responsibility for them whatsoever!

ALSO BY FRANCIS GILBERT

I'm A Teacher, Get Me Out Of Here (2004)
Teacher On The Run (2005)
Yob Nation (2006)
Parent Power (2007)
Working The System: How To Get The Very State Education For Your Child (2011)
The Last Day Of Term (2012)
Star-crossed: Romeo and Juliet for Teenagers (2013)
Gilbert's Study Guides on: *Frankenstein, Far From The Madding Crowd, The Hound of the Baskervilles , Pride and Prejudice, The Strange Case of Dr Jekyll and Mr Hyde, The Turn of the Screw, Wuthering Heights* (2013)

INTRODUCTION

I studied English Literature at the University of Sussex during the 1980s and then became an English teacher; I've been teaching in various secondary schools since 1990; I've taught A Level English for over two decades. In 2009, having taught full-time for many years, I went part-time at my school and embarked upon a PhD in Creative Writing and Education at an inner-city university. Since then, I've been lucky enough to teach English to undergraduates on a variety of different courses at different universities: some have been studying English as their main degree, but many have been taking a module which is about literature, while their main degree is another subject. I've found the experience fascinating but it's also made me realize that many undergraduates struggle to study English because it is such a difficult, open-ended subject which offers no simple answers to anything. I've encountered a number of students who've become very anxious and have been overwhelmed by the work-load. I've also met students who find it difficult having so much "free time" and have not been able to motivate themselves to work.

It's all made me realize that many students could benefit from a short guide which could point them in the right direction to getting a good degree either in English or scoring highly on an English module which forms part of another degree course. This book is suitable for both types of student.

I've designed this book so that it can be read quickly and can be dipped in and out of: the contents page is comprehensive. I've peppered it full of quotes from other students and broken up the text so that you can quickly scan through key points. It is aimed at anyone doing an English degree at university, or taking an English module in a Higher Education institution.

If you have any suggestions about how to improve this book, other comments or things you want to share with me, please email me: sir@francisgilbert.co.uk

Francis Gilbert, October 2013

WHY ENGLISH LITERATURE?

CASE STUDY: ANITA, AWAY FROM HOME

Anita arrived at university and felt completely overwhelmed by her new situation. It was the first time she'd ever stayed away from home; she was living in halls of residence in a big, busy city which intimidated her. She didn't know anyone. She joined in with the Freshers' Week but found the experience quite dispiriting; everyone else seemed to be having a great time and knew exactly what they were doing – and she didn't. Then the lectures and tutorials started; there were lots of handbooks and deadlines issued. Her head spun. She found that she didn't understand many of the lectures and was too frightened to speak up in seminars. After a few weeks into the course, she was already seriously thinking about dropping out. Why on earth had she chosen to study English? It had seemed easy at school, but at university it was much more complicated and there was so much more reading. She was feeling desperate.

What should Anita do?

Like all the case studies in this book, Anita is a "composite" of students I've encountered at university which reflect common situations I've seen firsthand myself; her situation is not rare.

There are quite a few things Anita should do. First, she needs to talk to someone about how she is feeling. The vast majority of universities have "counselors" who are trained to deal with problems like this, but every student will also have a personal tutor who should listen carefully if there are problems.

But there is a wider issue here as well and it's a central one for many English undergraduates; they don't quite know why they are doing a degree in the subject. Some students take English modules as part of another degree course; they sometimes have even deeper doubts. Many of them are good at English at school and have a love of the subject and they've "sort of drifted into it" or picked it because their intuition tells them they will enjoy it. They are not like medics or lawyers who have a set path from the get-go.

9

It's worth thinking therefore about WHY you're doing the course in order to get your "bearings"; you'll find that when things get tough, this will help you because you'll see the longer term goals you've set yourself and this could help motivate you to try harder – or just to keep going!

These are some quotes from students about why they've chosen to study English as a degree or as part of another degree course:

> "I chose English Literature as it considers all areas of life, languages, politics, history, nationalities etc, leaves you with a broad career scope and is relatively well-regarded."

> "Because I want to be an English teacher."

> "I have a passion for reading books."

> "I like discussing all the issues that literature raises."

Do any of these quotes ring bells? If not, write down your reasons for doing the course you're on: it will help you think about exactly why you've chosen to study English Literature.

It may be for purely intellectual reasons: you're fascinated by the subject; you love analysing literary texts; discussing and exploring them in depth; writing essays about them.

It may be for more practical reasons: you've found that you're good at it and you believe it will lead to you scoring highly for your degree ; it will assist with getting a good job and so forth.

Or it may be for emotional reasons; you just love reading and getting "lost" in literature.

Or possibly a mixture of all these things.

Take a minute to rank these statements and think about why you've chosen to study English Literature either as your main degree or as part of another degree:

- To analyse literary texts; to break them apart and see how they work.

- To have the chance to read a great many books in the literary canon.
- To become an English teacher.
- To become an academic.
- To get a job in the media such as publishing
- To learn and develop my essay writing skills.
- Having done this, what do you think you have learnt about yourself and your motivations?

SOME THOUGHTS ABOUT CAREERS

CASE STUDY: YOLANDA, DEPRESSED ABOUT CAREERS

Yolanda was depressed two years into her degree course because she felt that there were very few job opportunities open to her with an English degree and that teaching was the only realistic option. She knew that she definitely didn't want to teach. She'd done English because she was good at it at school and hadn't seriously thought about jobs, preferring to do something she was interested in. But now, with only a year to go, she was beginning to worry about what she could actually do. Unfortunately, she preferred to moan about the lack of opportunities on offer to her friends and worry privately rather than actually checking on the internet for openings or going to the careers' service. As a result, she procrastinated and didn't get anything fixed up when she'd finished her course.

What should Yolanda do? What should she have done?

Sadly, Yolanda's case is not uncommon. Many English graduates bury their heads in the sand about job opportunities and often scrabble around looking for a job when their course has finished. It is worth planning a bit ahead and realising that many of the myths about English degrees (or taking English as part of a degree) and the job market are not true. For example: did you know that English graduates have some of the best employment rates in the Europe and the US?

Although you may not have specifically chosen to English Literature to get a good job, this may well be at the back of your mind.

Quite a few students choose to study English because they want to become English teachers; many plan to do an English Literature degree and then complete a one year Post-graduate Certificate in Education (PGCE) or train on the job to teach English, which is an increasingly popular option. Other students want to work in the arts. Some want to become actors, screen-writers, or journalists.

One student, Grace, told me: "I want to be an actor and believe studying literature and the text is fundamental to understanding character." She was quite practical in her attitude; she knew that job prospects for actors weren't good so she planned to use the English degree not only to help with her developing her dramatic skills but also to get jobs along the way, such as working as an arts officer, or in advertising.

However, I've come across students who plan to use English as a stepping stone to a more traditional career in law, who will complete the degree and then do a conversion course to law when they've finished.

Most universities have excellent careers' services which will give you lots of advice about how to get the right job for you.

Even if you're in your first year, it's worth checking in them with them and having a discussion about your thoughts on a career; you may need some time to think about what you want to do. Added to which, you may want to get work experience in different areas during the holidays and they'll help you with that.

Website links:
http://www.prospects.ac.uk/options_english.htm
The Prospects website is a good place to begin to look at job opportunities; it contains lots of suggestions and some useful case studies as well.

THE TRANSITION FROM SCHOOL TO UNIVERSITY

CASE STUDY: JOSH, FROM TOP TO BOTTOM

Josh attended a school where he excelled at English; as a result, he always appeared to be the best student. Coming to university was a big shock because he felt like he was one of the worst in the year. During his first term, he received low marks for his essays and didn't do well in his exams. He found it very hard to adjust to the fact that he was expected to get on with most of the studying himself; there were no supervised reading classes, no clear instructions on how to write essays and very little guidance on taking exams. The lecturers seemed distant and cold compared with the friendly, positive English teachers he had at school. He began his second year feeling very depressed and was seriously considering dropping out of the course.

What should Josh do?

Well, first he needs to change his attitude about what to expect at university. Josh was expecting to receive the sort of one-on-one attention he enjoyed at school because he was one of the best. If he wants to get that, he needs to seek out lecturers and tutors for himself; he needs to be pro-active and ask them how he can improve. That, in his current depressed state, will take a real effort of will, but it needs to be done. A good place to start would be his personal tutor, or to speak to a tutor who he has found the most approachable. The jump from doing English at school to studying English at university is a big one. There are a number of differences.

Read these quotes from various undergraduates and think about whether any are relevant to you:

> "My teachers at school had a very narrow approach towards literature. At times it felt like they were trying to

just get you to hit the mark scheme and not enrich your experience."

"My experience at school was mostly boring and exam-focused. I learnt better by reading outside of school."

"English Lit at school was at a lot slower pace, which could be boring at times, but it meant we could do much more close analysis."

"Reading at school was very narrowly focused upon feminism."

"At school it felt easy and I loved my teacher. At uni I find there is a lot of support but some areas I have not enjoyed, in particular poetry as it was very technical. University depends mostly upon independent study and I am bad at this due to low self-esteem and procrastination as well as other commitments such as work."

First, you'll find you are much more on your own than you were at college or school. Typically while at school, you'll have had contact with one or two main English teachers and, if they were good teachers, you'll have had a great deal of guidance from them on all sorts of issues: what to read, how to write essays, how to study and prepare for exams. This sort of advice IS on offer at university, but YOU'RE GOING TO HAVE TO FIND IT FOR YOURSELF!

Generally speaking, tutors won't seek you out if you're falling behind with your work, nor chivvy you to write essays, or do the reading. You'll find very little finger-wagging of that kind. That said, if you fail to complete the basic requirements of the course, you may well be asked to leave so there is that ultimate sanction to bear in mind. If you do need help, you must go and ask for it.

This can take some courage, particularly if you don't know your tutors or lecturers that well. However, you'll find that most

English lecturers are surprisingly nice; there's more or less an "open door" policy at most universities and you should find you're warmly invited to discuss any issues you have with your tutors.

Next step: The student room website is an excellent place to log onto if you're finding your course difficult. You'll have a chance to connect with students in similar situations to you and find expert advice if you need it. http://www.thestudentroom.co.uk/ One huge difference you'll find at university is that there will be much less talk and discussion about exams in the seminars, lectures and tutorials. Students have consistently reported in surveys I have conducted that their A Level teachers were really focused upon exams, often to the detriment of the subject as a whole. One student said: "Teachers weren't enthusiastic, it's all about passing the exam. At university, it is very different, lecturers/tutors care about subject."

Exams are important on most English Literature degrees but you will find that there is comparatively little focus upon passing them in lectures and seminars. This is partly because of the way they are marked; you'll be expected to arrive at your original thoughts in an exam rather than meet specific criteria laid out in a highly prescriptive mark scheme.

PACE AT SCHOOL AND UNIVERSITY

The speed with which you cover topics is usually much faster than that found at school. As we will see when examining your reading load, you'll be expected to read at least 40-50 books in the year, usually spending a week on one text before moving onto another.

Next step: learn some speed reading techniques: http://www.speedreadingtechniques.com/

SCHOOL TEACHING VERSUS UNIVERSITY TEACHING

Read these quotes from English Literature students and consider your thoughts and feelings on their comments:

> "There were six students in our A Level English class: we were all very much involved and passionate about literature. My seminars remind me of these classes, but you rely much more on self-motivation."

> "Teachers weren't enthusiastic, all about passing the exam. At university, it is very different, lecturers/tutors care about subject."

> "I hated my sixth form, the teaching was condescending, boring, and they would not allow free thinking, it was all about passing the exam which they assured me I would not, BUT I LOVE IT HERE!"

At school or college, you may have had good or bad teachers, but whatever their quality, you probably got to know them quite well because you were taught by them for two or three hours a week over a two year course. It's unlikely you'll get to know a lecturer that well during your time at university; the relationship will probably be more impersonal. That said, you will have many more chances to see a wide variety of teachers not only in your scheduled lectures and seminars but also in additional events that are being held on campus. University is choc-a-bloc with extra curricula events where academics present their work. Go to some of them!

Above all, you need to remember that the lecturers at university are leading experts in their fields of expertise; teaching is just one aspect of their work. Much of the time, they are researching their subject in depth, writing books and papers, presenting their work at conferences and in the media.

One student said to me: "My A-Level English teacher was the most inspirational and passionate teacher I've ever had, he did nothing but encourage us all to engage with literature and do well. I haven't encountered anyone as good at university." I'm sure that this student was telling the truth, but I did want to tell him that they may be missing the point here; lecturers at university are passionate and inspirational about their work, but possibly don't see it as their primary duty to encourage students in the way an A Level teacher does.

GETTING HELP

You're much more on your own at university than at college or school. Everything is up to you and therefore it's vital that you do some things for yourself:

Get to know your personal tutor and TALK TO HIM OR HER, even if you're doing fine. Just tell them how you're getting on.

If you're struggling to attend courses or to do the work, you need to speak to either your personal tutor or the undergraduate secretary AS A MATTER OF URGENCY!!

The counselling services at most universities are excellent; you'll usually find an expert who is specially trained to talk you through any problems you may have.

If you're really feeling desperate, you can usually turn up without an appointment, but it is best to contact them first. Check your university's website for their contact details.

You can always speak the Samaritans if you just need someone to listen to your problems. I know it's a cliché but it is very true: a problem shared is a problem halved:

http://www.samaritans.org/

THE IMPORTANCE OF GOOD STUDY SKILLS

CASE STUDY: SACHA, ALWAYS ANXIOUS

Sacha found three things really bugged her doing her English degree: reading, note-taking and essay writing. She felt so stupid for being so worried about them. Surely she should know how to read books quickly and enjoy them? Surely she should know how to take proper notes? Surely she should know what a good essay looked like? She'd done well at school but she'd never had to do a lot of independent work; she'd read books for homework, but generally the teacher had provided her with good notes. She'd got good marks for her essays, but usually she'd been given clear guidance on how to structure those essays. Now she really felt like she'd been dropped in at the deep end: she did do the reading that was expected of her but it took her a very long time. She rarely socialized because she was usually working. She also did well with her essays but never quite understood WHY her essays were OK. She dreaded the day when she would be told that she had completed a bad piece of work. She was living in a state of constant anxiety.

What should she do?

First, Sacha needs to be aware of what is expected of her. Most of her worries stem from the fact that she doesn't quite know what is the normal workload. She needs to learn that she doesn't have to read every book in depth; sometimes it is entirely appropriate to use the contents page and index and "cherry-pick" the relevant quotes. She needs to take good notes, but not exhaustively detailed ones. With regard to essays, she could benefit from learning the different types of essays there are and experiment with writing in different styles to see which one suits her (see the chapter on "Essay Writing")

Second, she should be aware that she's not the only one! A great many English undergraduates are anxious because they are doing an important degree on a subject which is, let's face it, a bit "vague"; it's not science or mathematics where there are often clear answers. A great deal of English is based on opinion, backed up by evidence and argument; the people who do well are the ones that are the most articulate in shaping their arguments and analysis.

I made a short video with some of my students which explores some of these issues. You can find it here: http://www.youtube.com/watch?v=zKBjgmjyzGU

My research shows English Literature students consistently raise these big issues:

Reading and the note-taking related to reading. Many students find the amount of reading quite challenging.

Note-taking generally: in lectures, seminars, jotting down thoughts. Many students feel they don't know how to do this efficiently.

Dealing with seminars and lectures. Some students find seminars particularly stressful, especially if they are expected to give presentations or talk on the spot.

Essay writing. This is a major concern for students, quite a few of whom struggle to find their voice or know how to structure essays.

Exams. These seem to incur panic if not prepared for carefully.

Independent learning. This issue permeates everything you do at university. If you are someone who struggles to find the right motivation, who is bad at organising your time, who doesn't quite know how to structure your life, then you're going to find things difficult. This guide will attempt to provide some helpful, practical solutions and direct you to other sources where you might get even more help. This guide is going to look at each of these issues.

NOTE-TAKING

Good note-taking is vital. Whether you are doing this by hand or typing your notes into the computer, or dictating them, it is VITAL you have a good record of them.

Here are some comments from various students:

"Lots of reading done in the summer, it really helps to keep a term ahead and then quick revision of texts before lectures."

"Don't rely on lecturers to instill passion or enthusiasm! The more you read and research yourself the better and more interested you'll become."

"I found it difficult obtaining secondary reading. I was always unsure of what to read and spent a lot of time looking at irrelevant areas. The tutors were mostly very helpful however."

"The amount of books to read in the joint honours (English and Drama) at first was difficult to manage but after a few weeks I learnt to have a routine and know how many pages I can read in a week."

Above all, get organized: put your notes either into a proper book, or into folders. Personally, I like to read, scan and skim books, then write down my notes on the computer, saving them as a Word document.

Crucially, I write the name of the book, the author, the date of the publication, publisher at the top of the page and then make a table with TWO columns, using the TABLE facility in Word...

In the first column I write DIRECT QUOTES, in the second column, I write my opinions/thoughts. I find the TABLE very useful because it means that I don't mix up an author's quotations with my own.

I read novels, plays, poetry and drama differently from critical sources. I like to make time during the day to sit down and read this PRIMARY material properly, absorbing it, re-reading it.

Poetry is great because you can easily re-read it. I have a stack of poetry books by my bedside.

I am one of those people who has a few novels on the go at the same time. I'll read a few chapters and then perhaps switch to a new book. I buy the important texts so that I can highlight important passages, and then take notes later.

I like listening to key texts as well; many of them are on audio.

The key texts need to be READ and RE-READ, absorbed and thought about.

SECONDARY SOURCES

With English Literature, these are usually critical texts, commentaries by various literary critics and theorists about your primary texts. Sometimes, particularly in courses such as "Approaches To Literature" courses which examine literary theory, you'll be reading critical texts as a your primary sources, but mostly it'll be the works of criticism that have secondary importance. Indeed sometimes your tutors will much prefer you NOT to read the critics and come up with your own ideas about a primary source text because they won't want you to be too influenced by other critics' ideas. However, mostly you'll be expected to refer to other critics but in a CRITICAL FASHION!

I like to write out say FIVE or SIX important quotes from important critical books or articles. These quotes MAKE SENSE by themselves; i.e. I don't need to go back to the book to find out what the author meant.

As with primary sources, I divide my page into TWO, using the TABLE facility in Word, then I write the key quotations from my primary text on one side, and then questions/comments/observations on the other. That way I know what's a quote, and what's my thoughts. It's obviously absolutely vital that you don't confuse your own words with quotations from texts.

ORGANISING YOUR FILES

I love the computer because, being quite a disorganised person, I lose bits of paper. But on my computer I can easily be organised. First, I make folders for all the key course areas. Then within the key course areas, I make folders for the key texts or topics, then within those folders I place my notes/ideas/essays. I label all my files by putting the name of the book/article and the full date with year next to the file so that I know when I last worked on it. If I add to my notes, I update the date and put my old notes in a DISCARDED folder within this folder that way I never lose any of my notes.

REFERENCING

I must mention the importance of referencing at this point, because it will affect how you take your notes and how you write drafts of your essay. It's important to talk about it now because it's best to take notes/write drafts with referencing in mind.

There are several different systems of referencing available (e.g. Harvard, Chicago, MLA). The most widely used system used in the arts and humanities in the UK is that of the Modern Humanities Research Association (MHRA).

Some universities ask that you write in the Harvard style because it's regarded by some to be the simplest, clearest and most universally used form of referencing. This guide is written using the Harvard referencing style.

The main difference between the MHRA and Harvard is where you put the date. With MHRA you write:

Surname, First name, *Title in Italics or Underlined*. (Place: Publisher, Date) page numbers.

Larkin, Philip. *The Complete Poems*. (UK. Faber and Faber. 2012) p. 62

With the Harvard style you write:

Surname, Initial. (Date) Title in Italics or Underlined. Place Publisher. Page numbers.

Larkin, P. (2012) *The Complete Poems*. UK. Faber and Faber. p. 62

At the end of your essays, you MUST always put a bibliography which is a list of relevant books you have read for your essay or piece of research. This will be a list, in alphabetical order, of the books you have read which inform the essay.

The important thing is to be CONSISTENT and ACCURATE.

I cannot emphasize how important it is to get your referencing right; it immediately puts off anyone marking your work if it's obvious that you haven't used the correct referencing style. Above all, when you reference properly you show that you are acknowledging your sources, where your knowledge has come from.

Rather than list all the different styles here and how you should deploy them, you should read the relevant guide given to you by your university. THIS IS VERY IMPORTANT!!

LINKS FOR REFERENCING STYLES

The MHRA publishes the MHRA Style Guide, available as a free download from their website:
http://www.mhra.org.uk/Publications/Books/StyleGuide/download.shtml
This YouTube video made by the University of Derby is good on referencing in the Harvard Style:
http://www.youtube.com/watch?v=NDgqqPvMnoU
Anglia Ruskin University have produced a helpful webpage on using the Harvard style here:
http://libweb.anglia.ac.uk/referencing/harvard.htm

THE ANXIETY OF INFLUENCE: AVOIDING PLAGIARISM AND COMING UP WITH YOUR OWN IDEAS

Harold Bloom wrote a very influential book, *The Anxiety of Influence: A Theory of Poetry* (1997), which contained the key idea that writers are constantly using other people's work and re-shaping it for their own ends. Bloom's point is that writers are so aware that their work could be construed as imitations that they deliberately do something different. This key point needs to be thought about by you as you do your reading. As a burgeoning literary critic and writer, you will need to use other people's writing to formulate your own essays and thoughts, but you will need to avoid the trap of copying them directly. It's actually a delicate process.

Plagiarism, the copying of other people's work, is a huge issue in academia and you need to avoid it. Your department handbook should contain the basic rules and advice on this, but there are some other points to bear in mind as well.

There are two types of plagiarism; deliberate, willful cheating, and inadvertent, careless copying.

If you're an out-and-out cheat, there are a thousand ways to present someone else's work as your own. My experience is that I've never met an English graduate who is; the people who do cheat deliberately are usually desperate. They feel that that they need to get a top grade and, having so little confidence in their own abilities, they feel they need someone else to do the work for them. This is very sad. If you are feeling this way, you are probably feeling depressed and lacking in self-confidence. In which case, you need to go and speak to someone URGENTLY! It could be the College's counselling service, your personal tutor or even the Samaritans, but you do need to discuss this.

The main point is that you almost certainly will be found out sooner or later...All universities now have sophisticated software that detects plagiarism and all assessors are attuned at spotting it. It's usually pretty easy to discover for the trained eye. So don't do it! If you're caught and found guilty, your whole degree could be cancelled. It's just not worth the risk.

The second type of plagiarism is less reprehensible, but the consequences can be just as bad. If you've been sloppy about note-taking and haven't made clear distinctions between what is your work and another person's, then you could quite easily copy what you think is your notes into an essay and they are not! This needs to be avoided at all costs...

TAKING STEPS TO AVOID PLAGIARISM

Use decent source material: recommended books, recommended websites, particularly one that uses academically "peer-reviewed" such as JSTOR – in other words has been checked by other academics. Avoid Wikipedia, Spark Notes, or any other website that offers anonymous commentaries without references. Don't do everything in a rush. Take your time. Make sure you have time to read primary and secondary texts over a decent period of time so that you've got the 'head-space' to think things through. Plan things out so that you space out your reading and note-taking over a period of weeks or even months. Get your note-taking right. I suggested previously using columns to divide what a critic/writer says and what you say; you could, if you like, use different coloured pens, writing direct quotation in a different colour from your own thoughts. Whatever you do, it is VITAL that you know what is NOT your words, and what is.

NOTE-TAKING GENERALLY: IN LECTURES, SEMINARS AND ELSEWHERE

As an English student, the world is your TEXT! You may have important thoughts about the reading you are doing ANYWHERE! Be prepared, take a note-book with you everywhere and jot down your thoughts. Remember, the more you write, the better you become at it. Doing a little a lot is far better than trying to cram in lots of note-taking just before an essay or exam.

If you can, tape-record yourself or video yourself talking through points. Digital recorders are cheap now – many mobile phones have them – and they are good for taking notes when you've not got pen and paper to hand.

Get a reporter's notebook which is clearly labelled, putting the date when you started it on the front; this makes it useful to find stuff later on. Also, with reference to finding the relevant notes, make sure your notes are headed so that you know what CONTEXT the note has been taken in. Put quotes from lectures in quotation marks, different colours etc, so that you know YOU DID NOT SAY IT!! Jot down all the thoughts that come to you. Your thoughts while walking, cycling, having a coffee may be just as important as the ones you have in a more academic context. WRITE THEM DOWN IMMEDIATELY!! Don't try and take exhaustive notes in lectures. If you can, tape-record the lecture and listen carefully, jotting down the most important points. This way, you'll absorb the meaning of the lecture better.

Write down key points you've learnt immediately after a seminar, or ask for a few minutes at the end of the seminar to do this; most tutors will give you time to do this if you ask, and some may insist you do it anyway.

DEALING WITH SEMINARS AND LECTURES

CASE STUDY: JOHN, TOO SHY TO SPEAK?

John was a very clever student who was capable of writing some marvelous essays. However, he hated seminars, particularly when he had to give a presentation or answer a question asked by a tutor. He felt all the eyes of the students in the class were on him, waiting for him to trip up. Generally, he never spoke in seminars unless he really had to. A few months into his degree, he was finding that he didn't want to attend seminars at all because he thought he'd seen some students sniggering after he answered a tutor's question. It wasn't worth the stress. He started to skip seminars and then, finding it difficult to meet people, he failed to attend lectures; he was simply too shy to speak.

What should John do?

John is an extreme example of what I've seen a lot; very able students who just hate speaking in front of their peers or a lecturer for fear that they'll get something wrong. There's no easy answer to overcoming this problem; the thing is they may be right, some people might find it funny. Generally they don't, but it's always a problem.

The best way around the problem is to get into practice; learn to talk about literature with people you know well, or trust, run through presentations with them first. Get some support. If anxiety about this is really crippling you, you MUST SPEAK to your tutor, or go and see a counselor. As with reading, note-taking, and essay writing, it's all about practice, practice, practice...
This is a common problem; research shows that one of the biggest things that holds back students is their refusal to talk in seminars (Snapper, 2009).

USING THE WEB

CASE STUDY: MO, LOST ON THE INTERNET

Mo is addicted to his phone, and is constantly surfing the internet. When he settles down to work, he puts on Facebook, Twitter both on his phone and his laptop, and the surfs around looking for notes on the subject he is working on, viewing YouTube videos where relevant. He usually opens a Word document on his laptop and pastes notes into the document from the internet, except that he is not very systematic about this, and can forget to paste in the URL where the information comes from, and often fails to differentiate from his own notes and the notes he's copied from the internet. He uses Wikipedia a lot, and usually re-words what he's found there and uses that as the basis of his essay. At school, he did very well this way; using a mixture of his own words and more obscure stuff pasted from the internet, which his teacher didn't recognize. He was never stupid enough to copy anything he didn't understand, and usually re-words anything that doesn't sound like his voice. Since most of his essays are usually his own words, he doesn't have much of a problem with this. Added to which because he is usually on Facebook or Twitter when he is doing an essay in order to keep him motivated, he can become distracted and forget exactly what are his words and other people's. To begin with on his university course, he did well using this method; his work seemed good and clearly researched. However, he did very badly with his first coursework essay because he didn't acknowledge his sources and reference his work properly. In his second year, he was accused of plagiarism and had one piece of work disallowed, with the threat of being thrown off the course if he did it again. The trouble is that this chaotic way of working has become ingrained; he really finds he does NO WORK AT ALL if he is not on Facebook or Twitter; the social media motivates him to sit at the computer.

What should he do?

I think cases like Mo are more common than is generally acknowledged; lots of students I encounter spend long periods supposedly doing their essays when actually most of the time they are uselessly surfing the web. They think they are working, but they are not.

My personal advice is this: if you want to work on an academic essay/project properly, DO NOT LOOK at your emails first thing, DO NOT go on Facebook, or Twitter, unless it is to get help for your essay. Keep focused. Separate work from play.

Mo was doing some things right: pasting good quotes into a Word document from the internet is fine as long as you know they are quotes, and you have "cited" the sources by putting the relevant URL, author and date next to them.

But most importantly, don't fall into the Wikipedia trap! Use trusted sources, avoid Wikipedia to get your information – this is because Wikipedia can easily be tampered with and can provide false information. By all means use it as a first "port of call" but then check the references to see if they are correct. Most academics WILL NOT accept Wikipedia as a valid source of information if cited; you'll need to find it elsewhere.

An excellent place to start your explorations of the web is this link to a tour of the internet designed with English undergraduates in mind:

http://www.vtstutorials.co.uk/ws//tracking/launchconte
nt.aspx?cv=E33A8D48-DDA3-4F54-86F3-
A36A85BABD6A&e=A0000&c=26A1E896-9E85-416B-
83E3-952A5E946235&SID=6ea8c102-52cf-49de-95f9-
cf23aeffecfc

These are other websites that will prove invaluable:

- ✓ http://www.jstor.org/
- ✓ JSTOR is a not-for-profit organization which contains innumerable scholarly articles on a whole host of subjects. Your university will subscribe and you should be able to enter into the portal for free. Its search engine is good, but often it is best to type JSTOR into Google and then the name of the topic you want to get the best results. For example, if you want to find good articles on Jane Eyre, type in 'JSTOR, scholarly articles on Jane Eyre'. Google Scholar is also useful: it is easily accessed on the Google menu bar.
- ✓ http://www.intute.ac.uk/english/
- ✓ Although now not being updated, this website remains a useful place to find trusted resources for English, with links to lots of good scholarly articles.
- ✓ http://www.litencyc.com/
- ✓ *The Literary Encyclopedia* is an all-new reference work written by university teachers around the world. It is also a unique digital environment designed to integrate current knowledge of literature and culture and facilitate understanding of historical contexts and connections.
- ✓ http://literature.britishcouncil.org/
- ✓ Great, trusted information on contemporary writers as well as resources to help you understand challenging and thought-provoking literature.
- ✓ http://andromeda.rutgers.edu/~jlynch/Lit/
- ✓ Andromeda is a gateway to a wealth of resources/links designed to help English and American literature

undergraduates. Extremely useful, even if the design of the site is very basic.

✓ htt://vos.ucsb.edu/
✓ This is a fantastic site for learning about all the various literary theories and much, much more.

Discussion point

How do you use the internet to help you with your studies?

ATTITUDES TO READING

What do you think of these two comments made by English undergraduates?

> "Lots of reading done in the summer, it really helps to keep a term ahead and then quick revision of texts before lectures."

> "I've never got into a routine. How much I read varied from week to week depending on how interested I was in the text."

This honest comment from a student who struggled with the course is important to consider because she never got into a routine and only read what she wanted to. What do you think of this attitude? Do you secretly agree with her? Is that why you're on your English course: only really to read the books you like? Or do you have a different attitude towards reading?

Rank these comments and think about how you use your time

- o I enjoy reading for pleasure.
- o I enjoy reading for pleasure but not when I have to.
- o I am not a great reader.
- o I am looking forward to reading all the set texts on my reading list.

- o I will set aside time to read the set texts every day, making sure I do at least one-two hours reading a day.
- o I am feeling positive about some texts, but I know I will give up on texts I don't find immediately easy.
- o I will persevere with difficult texts, using study guides to help me if necessary.
- o My English teacher mostly guided me through difficult texts.

It's vital that you reflect upon what your attitudes towards reading actually are. Be honest with yourself. If you know that you've never actually read a "difficult" text by yourself but always had a teacher explain the key aspects of it to you, you're going to find the course quite difficult. You're going to need to find some strategies to help you with this (see below). If you're someone who is rather "random" about when and what they read, you're going to need to be disciplined about setting aside time to read.

Discussion points

What are your reading habits? What are your attitudes towards reading? What texts do you expect to study on the course? What would you hope to study? Wordsworth once famously said: "we murder to dissect". Do you think this is true of literature? Share your thoughts – see up a discussion forum on the internet if you like...

YOUR EARLY READING AND WRITING EXPERIENCES

Philip Larkin famously said "books are a load of crap" in his poem, *A Study of Reading Habits* (p.62) despite the fact that he was a famous poet, worked as a university librarian and read voraciously. Have there been times when you have had a similarly negative attitude towards reading? When and why? Larkin is admittedly being ironic, but his central argument in the poem is a strong one: books become tired over time, they don't represent the reality of the world, and they stop you from living your life. Do you wish you were actually "living your life" rather than reading? Or do you think making these sorts of divisions are false?

It's worth reflecting upon your own reading experiences and thinking about what your underlying attitudes towards reading and writing are because they will inform how you read and write on this course. The researcher Deborah Brandt conducted some seminal research in her survey *Literacy in American Lives* (2001) and showed that many people have very different attitudes reading and writing. Often parents helped their children to read but not to write and, because of this, attitudes towards reading and writing are quite different. Brandt found that reading was often associated with being at home, while writing was associated with being at school. This may have changed with the development of new platforms for writing such as mobile phone texting, social media and the internet generally.

FURTHER READING

Deborah Brandt *College Composition and Communication* , Vol. 49, No. 2 (May, 1998), pp. 165-185, Published by: National Council of Teachers of English
Article Stable URL: http://www.jstor.org/stable/358929

COPING WITH THE READING

What kinds of literature do you really like? What writers do you like and why?

> "In general, close reading of language is the ultimate key skill. Moving away from A Level approach of character analysis and searching for 'meaning/intention' has been difficult..."

You probably have chosen this course because you feel a deep affinity, even love for, certain types of literature.

Having thought about this, do you think it's really possible to "love" a piece of literature? What processes go on in your mind that make you really love it? Are you able to empathise, for example, with certain characters or situations in certain texts? Crucially, do you think the texts you love can love you back? Is the feeling in any way reciprocal? This may sound like a stupid question but sometimes feelings run very high with literature; sometimes people do "bond" very strongly with certain texts and do feel, in certain ways, that the author, or the text, is speaking to them. This is perhaps most vividly seen with religious texts such as the Bible, but it can happen with other texts as well.

These sorts of feelings for literature are great, but you will have to form other relationships with texts during this course. Yes, there will be texts that you "love", but there will be also ones that you are frustrated by, confused by, even downright angry at. You may well feel a "loss of self" as you leave behind your personal response to literature and enter a more academic "discourse" – a mode of address, of talking. This is a discourse that has, by and large, developed in the last hundred and fifty years and it's worth investigating how and why it evolved before you commence properly with your studies.

DEVELOPING INDEPENDENCE

Put these statements in rank order with the ones you agree most with at the top.

- Being independent is a state of mind which involves feeling confident that you can do things by yourself.
- Being independent is difficult when you're worried about things unconnected with your work such as money-worries or problems with relationships.
- Being independent means developing your own routine and sticking to it.
- Being independent means that you can read most texts and understand them immediately.

- Being independent means you work hard on understanding concepts that you find difficult.
- Being independent means you can ask for help when you need it.

This questionnaire is also useful: http://www.prepareforsuccess.org.uk/studying_indep endently.html

The issue of working independently is probably the most important factor in determining how well you do at university. On an English course, all these types of independence are important, although it's independence with reading and writing that play the biggest role in how successful you are.

GETTING INTO THE HABIT OF WRITING

One of the best ways you'll improve in all areas connected with English is by writing a sort of "diary" or log book, which is not only a personal diary but also is a place where you jot down your own informal thoughts on the texts you are studying and the ideas you are formulating in your head.

Exciting new research (http://www.thinkingwriting.qmul.ac.uk/) suggests that we think differently when we write things down and that writing has a way of sequencing, ordering, refining and constructing thoughts that is quite different from those thoughts that arise through discussion or just "thinking in your head".

Get a notebook and date it on the front, dating your entries as you go along.

Write down your thoughts and feelings about coming on the course; your ambitions; your fears and your hopes.

You can use this logbook as the "source book" for your studies if you wish. Write down any thoughts you have about books you are reading; take a note of titles of books, year of publication, authors, write down interesting quotes, your musings on the book. Write down your reflections upon lecturers and seminars you have attended.

There's a marvelous lecturer Les Back, a Professor in Sociology at Goldsmiths College, University of London, who has written a brilliant "academic diary" which is worth a look; he's published it online and used it as a way of merging his personal and academic life: http://www.academic-diary.co.uk/

Why not set up your own blog like Les Back's?

Obviously, you should leave out any personal stuff that you're uncomfortable with sharing with the world (remember your blog is publicly available to EVERYONE) but perhaps include personal responses to literature that don't compromise you or anyone else.

CASE STUDY: JOE, NOT BRIGHT BUT ORGANISED

Joe had attended a very academic, highly selective school and was pushed hard by his parents to achieve. Being in such a "hothouse" made Joe aware that there were a great many people much cleverer than he was – and harder working. However, Joe developed a strategy for dealing with this; he was organized. He always met deadlines, he always filed his notes carefully, always put his work into clear folders on the computer, always listened carefully. At the beginning of the year, he entered all the important deadlines on a calendar which he pinned to his wall. He wasn't aiming to get top marks, and settled for a solid 2.1, which was more than his teachers at school expected him to get. He achieved this good degree not through talent or even working that hard, but by being organized. Unlike his more talented colleagues, he never missed a seminar, a lecture or a deadline. He always had done the reading. He did more or less the minimum of what was expected, but he always did it. At the beginning of every day, he would set himself targets as to what he was going to do during that day, and he stuck to the targets. This way he found he could have a great social life, and get the work done.

Why did Joe succeed where many other failed? The answer is simple, he kept on top of the work by setting himself clear targets and goals. It's a very obvious point, but it illustrates the virtues of getting organized. Target setting is very useful in this regard; either in the evening, or the morning, set yourself some goals for the day. Don't be too unrealistic; make them modest if you know that you want to go out or do something else. But set them, and then carry them out: the first thing to do is to get your head around where you are headed!

YOUR COURSEWORK DEADLINES, YOUR EXAM DATES

Check these out in your Handbook/Department guide now – if you haven't already done so! Write them down in your diary, in your calendar, in your phone, tattoo them in your brain! Even early on in a course, it's worth looking at whether there are any deadlines that are "bunched together"; you may have some major assignments to hand in within days of each other with LOTS of reading for each one of them. It's worth thinking about this now and thinking about when you might begin on them. Obviously, you're not going to write them immediately, but you may well think that it's perhaps wise to start doing the reading and research for them some months before the actual deadline, instead of a few panic-stricken days before they're due...

Other essay deadlines. These are not coursework essays – you're not formally assessed on them for your degree – but they are usually MANDATORY; in other words, you HAVE TO DO THEM! Often you will be given a "classification" for them, and you'll feel bad if you don't really make an effort.

Exams. Most of these take place in May but check your department handbook.

UNDERSTANDING LITERARY THEORY

Many students feel tense when they hear the words "literary theory" – and quite a few academics too – but I believe getting to grips with "literary theory" is vital if you're going to get the most out of your English degree and most English modules. Literary theory has a bad name because some of it is written in a very difficult style and can be hard to understand. There are a few things to consider before we look at this topic in depth. First, it's worth thinking about what literary theory is. This is a difficult, thorny topic in itself. Literary theory is NOT like scientific theory; it often is much more philosophical in its approach, it doesn't have specific hypotheses which can be tested by experiments. Instead, it usually contains speculations, thoughts, ideas, arguments about WHY texts have been written, WHY and HOW we use language, and WHAT goes into the processes of reading, writing, speaking and listening.

A SHORT HISTORY OF READING AND WRITING

You could argue that the human brain "reads" the world. When you were first born, you saw nothing, your eyes weren't focused in any way, but you knew instinctively when you were hungry. As you developed, your brain learnt that certain sounds represented certain people such as your mother. Your eyes learnt to "read" or "decode" the world around you; your brain actively constructed and gave meaning to what you saw. Some thinkers like Derrida argue that the whole world is a "text" that we read (Glendinning, 2011).

Then, when you were old enough, you started to read books, which enabled you to make links between signs on a page, sounds in people's mouths and specific things in the world around you. Such an experience is relatively new in terms of human evolution.

Historians believe that reading and writing developed ten thousand years ago in the Middle East and even then it was only a tiny educated elite who were able to read. It was perceived as a religious activity that put people in touch with the word of God in a number of different religions and cultures.

The advent of printing increased the number of people who read immensely and changed the face of the world as a consequence. You could argue that religious reformations, revolutions, and massive social change was the direct result of the printing revolution. The "common" people had access to information which was normally only read by a tiny elite.

Similarly, some thinkers suggest that the internet is leading to similar upheavals throughout the world because it has hugely widened people's access to information once again.

And yet, the elites do remain! Even in a democratic country like the UK, only a fraction of the population own most of the wealth and, by and large, all the top professions are stuffed full of people from the most prosperous backgrounds. In other countries, it's even worse with a mere handful of people owning and controlling everything, while the rest of the population lives in abject poverty.

The truth is that while being able to read and write used to be a way out of poverty and ignorance, so much more is expected now. It is assumed that everyone will be literate. The question now is HOW literate they are: the extent of their reading, the quality of their writing. This is why things like studying English Literature at university have developed, they afford people the chance to extend their literacy skills way beyond the common man. They give their students what the French sociologist Pierre Bourdieu calls "cultural capital"; the symbolic tools of the elite. In other words, courses like English Literature give students access to powerful symbolic codes which enable them to ultimately gain power and prestige in society. The universities, in his view, are more about securing the power of the elite classes than really educating...

Discussion points

Why has reading and writing become so important in our society? Is Bourdieu right, do universities reinforce the values of the dominant classes?

GOOD LINKS FOR DEVELOPING YOUR READING

http://www.bl.uk/learning/langlit/timeline/index.html
http://www.bl.uk/learning/langlit/index.html
http://www.poetryfoundation.org/
http://www.poetryarchive.org/poetryarchive/home.do

USEFUL READING:

Lyons, M. (2009) *A History of Reading and Writing In the Western World* Palgrave Macmillan.

WHY WRITE?

When you think about it, putting lots of marks on bits of paper or onto a screen is a bit weird; there's something rather surreal about writing and reading. However, there is something magical as well in the sense that knowledge can be conveyed so succinctly and preserved supposedly forever by these marks. Nevertheless, it's not hard to see the futility in it all. Why aren't we all going out and enjoying ourselves instead? There's no doubt at times you'll feel like this on this course because you'll have worked so closely with the written word, both reading and writing it. This said, it's worth considering the power of the written word. I'd like to dwell upon two aspects of the written word: its role in communicating in a private, personal sphere, and its role in communicating in a public realm:

As a tool for personal, private reflection; for communicating with the self; for expressing one's innermost thoughts and desires. The written word gives you access to your inner-most thoughts in a way that no other form of communication can. Seeing those words emerge on the page in front of you as you write your diary expressing your emotions, your thoughts, your ideas about the world is, when you think about it, quite remarkable. It is your mind made manifest. This is possibly why people become so attached to their diaries and journals. They are an extension of the self. As an English student, you'll be examining writing which either is this form of autobiographical writing, or represents it. For example, in a Shakespeare play, soliloquies give us access to his characters' innermost thoughts and desires, while the novel itself arose because writers like Defoe and Richardson fictionalised personal letters or diaries. The primary purpose of the writing is to represent the inner workings of individual minds; to reflect upon the world from the standpoint of the individual person.

As a tool for informing, persuading and analysing; as a very public tool for communication. When I spoke about writers such as Shakespeare using the written word to express private emotions and ideas, I was conscious that his language operates also in the public realm as well. It is very much language designed for public performance. It is, at once, private and public. Because literature's role is often, though not always, about communicating publicly to an audience or readership. This, for me, is what makes literature so unique; it operates simultaneously in the private and public realms. It expresses many private thoughts, but is aired publicly. It is in many cases very consciously there to be scrutinised by the public; it often has an informative and persuasive role. It aims to change people's minds about certain issues or concepts. This said, it is often not "analytical"; it doesn't seek to critique an issue in the way that a philosophical essay or piece of literary criticism might.

GOOD LINKS FOR LEARNING MORE ABOUT WRITING

http://www.bl.uk/learning/artimages/why/why1/whydo wewrite.html
http://www.bl.uk/learning/artimages/why/ways1/wayso fwriting.html

A History of the Study of English Literature

The Great Tradition

You could argue that it was a group of lecturers at Cambridge University during the 1920s that gave the study of English Literature its academic footing (Young, pp. 25-26). Until then, the study of literature had very much been the province of informed gentleman, journalists and writers. Many authors from the Romantic and Victorian era, including Blake, Wordsworth, Coleridge and possibly most significantly, Matthew Arnold, wrote criticism and cultural commentaries on the role of literature in society, much of which is still very pertinent today. However, there was no drive to make the study of literature a scientific discipline; indeed much of their writing was a reaction against the scientific method.

But the Cambridge lecturers, led by I.A.Richards were determined to show that literature could be studied scientifically. Richards pioneered a method called "practical criticism" which involved analysing poetry in great depth by taking the poem out of its context and looking very carefully at the linguistic devices it deployed. You were probably taught a version of practical criticism at school, when you may have looked exhaustively at a poet's use of alliteration, onomatopoeia, rhyme and rhythm in a piece of coursework or exam.

Richards and his colleagues, who included critics from America as well, believed very strongly that some literary texts were far better than others in their use of literary devices. This fundamental belief in a hierarchy of texts led to the establishment of a "literary canon" in the academic realm with certain writers such as Chaucer and Shakespeare being accorded much higher status than most others. Richards' follower, F.R. Leavis (1895-1978) took things even further in his book *The Great Tradition* by singling out certain novelists – like Jane Austen, George Eliot, Henry James and Joseph Conrad – as being "great", while more popular forms of fiction was dismissed as being worthless (Young, pp. 25-26). His central argument was that certain texts are so good that they transcend their time because they contain timeless characters and truths. Although Leavis did choose some women to be part of the canon like Austen and Eliot, most of his choices were dead white men (Pope, p. 137).

From the 1980s, many academics have questioned the whole concept of the literary canon, doubting whether one can create a hierarchy of texts in this way, asking whether there are "timeless truths" embedded in texts like messages in a bottle (Eagleton, 1996a).

What do you think? As a result of their questions, new texts emerged as worthy of study: popular fiction, genre fiction, experimental writing, writing by women, writing by people from a variety of different cultures and ethnic backgrounds. Furthermore, different ways of reading texts emerged. These can be extremely confusing, particularly when you're tackling them for the first time. Unfortunately, if you're really engaging with different approaches to reading texts, you will be confused!

However, I've found that if you break down these approaches into certain key areas, then you find that there are common points between all of them. Let's look at the different areas that different approaches to literature take:

Contexts of writing. You'll find many lectures about literature at university contextualise a literary text, that is, they place a text in the time when it was written; the lecture will possibly explore the life of the author and how that influenced the writing of the text; it may look at the society that the text emerged from and how the values of that society shaped and influenced the language of the text; it could look at the ways in which other texts influenced the writing of the text. The main point is that what is being explored is the background to the writing of the text; the different contexts it emerged from. In my experience, this is the most common form of lecture that you'll find in most university English Literature departments. They are fascinating lectures because you'll be given a real over-view of how and why the text was written. At university, you're really lucky because you'll hear experts discuss literary texts; often they will give you a brilliant insight into how writers came to create seminal texts. This is a very broad area and critics who take different approaches can use their particular approach or interest to inform how they present the contexts in which a text was written. For example, a Marxist critic may well examine how the social structure of the period shaped and influenced the writing of a text, while a psycho-analytical critic may look at the sexual morals of the time and consider how attitudes towards sexuality informed the text (Castle, Pope, pp. 164-66).

Contexts of reading. This is an approach which is not so common as examining the contexts of writing of a text and possibly more contentious, but, for me, makes profound sense. This approach considers the different ways in which a reader reads a text and examines the way in which a reader's social class, gender, age, ethnicity, geographical and historical location influences the reading of a text. As its starting point, it asserts that a text only has meaning in the mind of a reader; that readers construct the meaning of a text in their head and that depending upon their background or context, they'll read a text differently from another person. For example, with a Shakespeare play like *Othello*, someone who is black may well have different perspectives on the racist language in the play than someone who is white. Similarly, a woman may view the abuse that Desdemona suffers from in the play quite differently from a man. Furthermore, a person who is from a society that denies the rights of women may well make different observations than someone who comes from a society where women are more equal.

A large body of theory has developed around this approach with the two leading lights being Stanley Fish (Pope, p. 274), who helped developed what is now known as the "Reader-Response" theory, and Stuart Hall (Eagleton, 1996b), a theorist who shaped what is known as "Reception Theory" which is widely used on Media Studies courses, but is equally applicable to English Literature students.

Other approaches that examine the "contexts of reading" of a text are structuralists who look very carefully at how language creates effects in readers' minds (Pope, 175). They are far less concerned about the wider contexts of reading and much more interested in how and why language creates certain connections and contrasts in a reader's mind. This was probably an approach you were taught at school.

Unfortunately, when it's taught in a moribund fashion, it can kill a text because you end up "feature-spotting", looking in dry fashion for the various linguistic techniques in a text such as alliteration, onomatopoeia, personification, the use rhyme and rhythm and so forth, with your mind desperately trying to find a suitable effect to go with the technique. This said, if done well, it's a very illuminating and inspiring approach. At your university, you'll find experts in many of these fields, and you'll find that you are inspired by their fantastic close reading of various poems, plays and novels.

Many theorists can be slotted within these two categories: critics who examine the "contexts of writing" (the circumstances of the writing of the text) and those who address the "contexts of reading" (how readers interpret the text) texts.

Next step: Read *Living Literature* (2000) pp. 42-80. This is an A Level text book but it contains the best and clearest explanation of these tricky theoretical issues I've found.

SOCIAL CLASS AND MARX

Many critics from different fields examine the role of social class in shaping a text. The most notable critics who analyse texts from this perspective are usually heavily influenced by Marxism (Pope, pp. 155-63).

Karl Marx was a nineteenth century philosopher who theorised that the most decisive factor in society was social class. He divided society up into the working classes (the proletariat), the middle-class (the bourgeoisie), and the upper classes (the aristocracy, or the ruling class).

His contention was that the bourgeoisie and the upper classes enjoyed most of the profits of the work done by the proletariat. He suggested to overcome this situation, the working classes should join together and overcome the ruling elite by force, and then establish their own communist state where all the profits of labour were divided equally between all people (Singer, p. 33).

A Marxist critic examines literary texts from this perspective, looking at the ways in which social class is represented in a text. There are two key approaches. The Marxist critic who actively searches for other overtly Marxist texts, or the critic who looks at texts which may not be Marxist in outlook but examine the role of social class (Pope, 155-63). Critics who take slightly different approaches such as cultural materialists also do this (Pope, p. 160).

POST-STRUCTURALISM

There are a whole host of other literary theorists who could come under the umbrella of being post-structuralist critics or thinkers. The term "post-structuralism means "after structuralism" and has been a label applied to theorists who have either rejected or developed the concepts of structuralism. Structuralism started as a social science and was used by anthropologists like Levi-Strauss to categorize and analyze social groups by looking at the ways in which they deployed "binary opposites" in their language and culture. Structuralists theorized that language and culture developed through the use of opposites; that many words are defined by what they are NOT. So light wouldn't exist as a concept without darkness, its opposite. Likewise, "good" wouldn't be a moral quality without the notion of "evil".

A key figure in the development of these ideas was the French thinker, Roland Barthes (1915-1980), who wrote an essay, *Death of the Author* (Belsey, p. 18), which is studied on most English degree courses because it is so influential. Barthes put the case that the intention of an author can never be fully known, that language is slippery and full of different shades of meaning, connoting different things to different people, depending upon their context.

Other thinkers such as Michel Foucault and Jacques Derrida took things even further, arguing that subjectivity and the notion of the individual author is an illusion, a social construct, and that there are only "discourses" – ways of talking and writing – which permeate texts. Unlike Leavis and other more traditional critics, who developed the cult of the author, Derrida and Foucault examined the underlying contextual meanings of texts, looking at the ways in which they promoted certain ideas and examining why those ideas were there. They often wrote in a complex way because they were trying to escape from the constraints of ordinary language, trying to invent a new way of thinking about texts and ourselves. (Belsey, p. 42, p.56)

Many feminist critics have deployed a poststructuralist outlook because they've seen it as a way of deconstructing the underlying gender assumptions that underpin much of our language and literature. Feminist critics such as Catherine Belsey and Gayatri Spivak have looked at the ways in which our language endorses male power.

At university, you'll find lecturers exploring many different approaches to texts. It's well worth getting your head around the different theories though during your first year. There are some brilliant, clear and lucid books that explain everything quite clearly.

In the next chapter, there is a summary of the basic historical periods in literature, together with questions and next steps to help understand how texts exhibit the traits of these periods.

USEFUL READING ON LITERARY THEORY

Castle, G. (2013) *The Literary Theory Handbook (Blackwell Literature Handbooks)* Wiley-Blackwell.

I found this guide very readable; Castle takes you through all the basic literary theories in an insightful and engaging fashion. The book is expensive so make sure you get it out from the library.

Eagleton, T. (1996) *Literary Theory – An Introduction* Wiley-Blackwell.

This book has become a seminal text – far more than a study guide -- in itself with Eagleton not only offering advice on how to read and apply literary theory but also providing some of his own provocative, witty insights into various approaches. He is always readable but can quite intellectually challenging and personally I would read Castle or Pope before tackling his book, which is essential but difficult at times.

He's a good speaker and can be found here delivering a brilliant lecture on the death of criticism:
http://www.youtube.com/watch?v=-2odZxUAfuo&feature=related

Pope, R. (2012) *Studying English and English Literature.* Routledge.

If you buy one expensive book on your course which may not be on your reading list, buy this one! It really is a cornucopia of information and help. Pope is an eminent literary critic and a really sensible voice of authority; this book is very detailed and useful, providing in-depth guidance on how to analyse literary and non-literary texts, as well as clear explanations of a host of literary theories and approaches. The book also provides very useful web links as well.

LITERATURE YOU REALLY NEED TO KNOW ABOUT

THE BIBLE

Why do you need to know about *The Bible* to be a good English Literature student? Surely, it's a religious text? Well, yes, it is, but it is also possibly the most influential literary text ever written. Until comparatively recently, the Bible influenced every English writer because it was the main text most people listened to and read since most writers had Christian upbringings.

The Bible is divided into two sections: *The Old Testament* and *The New Testament*. *The Old Testament* forms the Torah for the Jewish religion, but also the first part of the Christian Bible. It is a collection of stories, the first of which was possibly written down in 3500 BC and drawn together by religious scholars over the ages. For the purposes of the English Literature student, the most important edition of the Bible is the *King James Version* or *Authorised King James' Version* **(AKJV)** or **(KJB)** published in 1611. This English translation of the Bible is widely considered to be the most beautiful and is certainly the most influential; phrases it uses are often quoted in much succeeding literature. You can find it online here:

http://www.kingjamesbibleonline.org/1611-Bible/

A more comprehensible version is the New International Version (NIV), which lacks the poetry of the AKJV but is easier to understand.

GENESIS: THE CREATION OF EARTH

In a nutshell: God makes the universe, earth, animals and humans in seven days.

Key quote, **Genesis**, **chapter 1, verse 1 (AKJV)**: "In the beginning God created the heavens and the earth. Now the earth was formless and empty, darkness was over the surface of the deep, and the Spirit of God was hovering over the waters."

GENESIS: THE STORY OF THE GARDEN OF EDEN

In a nutshell: God creates Adam, the first man, and then Eve, from Adam's rib, as a mate for Adam. He allows Adam and Eve to roam freely in Eden -- the paradise he has created -- but forbids them to eat from the tree of knowledge. Eve is persuaded by the serpent (the devil or Satan) to eat the fruit from the tree of knowledge by saying that she will become as knowledgeable as God. Eve eats the apple and then persuades Adam to eat it too so that they are equal. God sees that they are covering up their nakedness and that they are ashamed. He knows that they've eaten from the tree. He punishes them by ordering that men will have to work very hard to have enough to eat, women will always suffer in childbirth and humans will die. He makes the serpent crawl on its belly.

Key quote: Genesis, chapter 3, verse 16: To the woman God said, "I will make your pains in childbearing very severe; with painful labour you will give birth to children. Your desire will be for your husband, and he will rule over you."

Influences: This is one of the most influential stories ever written and is constantly referenced in poetry, plays and novels. St Augustine interpreted this story as meaning that everyone born after Adam and Eve is born into sin because their sin has been passed on to all their descendants. He called this "original sin": this is a very important idea in Christianity and many Christians still believe in it as a concept. However, non-conformist Christian writers like William Blake (1757-1827) rejected the idea as being deeply oppressive. Look for references to "forbidden fruit", paradise, original sin.

NOAH AND THE FLOOD

In a nutshell: God is angry with mankind and kills them all with a flood, except for Noah who he tells to make a boat and put his family and all the animals on it.

Key quote: Genesis, chapter 7, verse 6 (AKJV): "Noah was six hundred years old when the floodwaters came on the earth. And Noah and his sons and his wife and his sons' wives entered the ark to escape the waters of the flood. Pairs of clean and unclean animals, of birds and of all creatures that move along the ground, [9] male and female, came to Noah and entered the ark, as God had commanded Noah."

Influences: The idea of "Armageddon", of escaping from danger, of preserving life is central to countless texts.

THE TOWER OF BABEL

In a nutshell: The people of earth speak one language and build a huge tower, the tower of Babel, which reaches to the heavens to show how powerful they are. God, annoyed that they are trying to be like him, destroys the tower and makes everyone speak a different language so that they don't understand each other.

Key quote: Genesis, chapter 11, verse 6(AKJV): The LORD said, "If as one people speaking the same language they have begun to do this, then nothing they plan to do will be impossible for them. Come, let us go down and confuse their language so they will not understand each other."

ABRAHAM & ISAAC

In a nutshell: God gives Abraham a covenant (a holy promise) and tells him that the Jewish people will become slaves of another people, but then will be rescued by God. Abraham is told to sacrifice his son, Isaac, to prove his obedience to God; Abraham gets his son ready to kill him, but suddenly a heifer or goat appears and God tells him that he can sacrifice that instead; Abraham's son is saved because Abraham had proved his worth.

Influences: The idea of doing your duty even though it harms you and your family is a central theme of many texts.

JOSEPH AND HIS BROTHERS

In a nutshell: Joseph was a favourite son of Jacob and was given a lovely, multi-coloured coat by Jacob. Joseph has strange dreams about the corn and the stars bowing down to him. When he tells his brothers about these, they are jealous, and are jealous of his coat. The brothers plot to kill him but are persuaded by the eldest brother Reuben to throw him into a pit. Then some merchants come by and the brothers take Joseph's coat and sell him to the merchants. He was taken to Egypt, fell out with the merchant and was imprisoned. But news came to the Pharaoh of Joseph and his strange dreams. Joseph tells his dreams to the Pharaoh which warn of famine and tells him to store grain so that the country is prepared. Joseph becomes a Governor because the Paraoh is so pleased with him. Meanwhile, his brothers are starving in Canaan. Joseph realises they have changed and rescues them, bringing them to live with him in Egypt.

Influences: Apart from spawning a musical, this story has been re-interpreted many times. The central motif of the abject slave becoming very powerful, ascending from the bottom of the social ladder to the top is common in many stories.

SODOM AND GOMORRAH

In a nutshell: people were behaving very badly in Sodom and Gomorrah, having sex with people they supposedly shouldn't have sex with, possibly having homosexual sex so God destroyed the city and killed all the inhabitants with fire and brimstone.

Influences: These names are still synonymous with concepts of sexual depravity.

MOSES IN "EXODUS" THE NEXT BOOK IN THE BIBLE AFTER GENESIS

In a nutshell: Moses hears God speaking from a burning bush saying that he will rescue the Jewish people from slavery in Egypt. Moses leads the Jewish people out of Egypt, known as the Exodus (listen to the Bob Marley song) to the promised land, Israel – which is the name of God, who is also known as Elohim and Jahweh, his name though is spelt out fully in Jewish literature.

Called by God to Mount Sinai, God gives Moses the Ten Commandments, vital rules that must be obeyed.

Key quote: Exodus 20:1-17 (AKJV) "And God spake all these words, saying, I *am* the LORD thy God, which have brought thee out of the land of Egypt, out of the house of bondage. Thou shalt have no other gods before me. Thou shalt not make unto thee any graven image, or any likeness *of anything* that *is* in heaven above, or that *is* in the earth beneath, or that *is* in the water under the earth: 5 thou shalt not bow down thyself to them, nor serve them: for I the LORD thy God *am* a jealous God, visiting the iniquity of the fathers upon the children unto the third and fourth *generation* of them that hate me; and shewing mercy unto thousands of them that love me, and keep my commandments."

Influences: much literature explores the consequences of rules and regulations.

SAMSON AND DELILAH

In a nutshell: For forty years the Israelis suffered at the hands of the Philistines, a terrible enemy who lived near the sea. However, a mighty warrior Samson was born who not only could kill lions, but also Philistines. Samson fell in love with a beautiful woman called Delilah who was secretly working for the Philistines; she discovers the secret to his strength is his long hair. When he was asleep, she signalled to the Philistines to cut off his hair; Samson was captured and blinded, and taken to Gaza where he was thrown in prison. The Philistines celebrated their triumph in their temple and brought out the blinded prisoner to highlight their victory; he was put between the pillars of a doorway so that everyone could see him. The crowd jeered at how weak he was. Asking the Lord for help, Samson pushed the pillars on either side of him over making the temple collapse, killing everyone inside, including himself.

Influences: A tremendously influential story. Delilah is the original "femme fatale"; the woman who leads a great man to his doom. The story of the injured, weakened warrior who has one last victory has influenced numerous stories from King Arthur to James Bond.

DAVID AND GOLIATH

In a nutshell: Weedy but clever David defeats Goliath in a fight by being clever and using a sling-shot to hit him with stones. David becomes King and marries Bathsheba after making her pregnant and causing her husband's death by sending him to fight in a battle.

Influences: Hardly a day goes by when this story isn't referenced in one or another. It is an archetypal story in that it shows how brains beat brawn.

KING SOLOMON'S WISDOM

In a nutshell: The son of David, King Solomon was asked by God in a dream what he most wanted and he replied "wisdom". One day, two mothers came to him claiming that a baby was theirs and asking Solomon to decide who was the real mother. Solomon got out his sword and said he would cut the baby in two and give them half each. One of the women said this was a good idea, while the other broke down in tears and said that she would rather the other woman had the baby than see the child killed. Solomon then knew she was the mother. After this story, people realized he had the wisdom of God.

Influences: The idea of the wise ruler or the wise man appears in many stories such as Prospero in Shakespeare's *The Tempest* to Thomas Cromwell in Hilary Mantel's *Wolf Hall*.

THE NEW TESTAMENT -- THE GOSPELS

In a nutshell: These four books were written by Mark, Luke, Matthew and John. They are all about the life of Jesus and contain similar stories about him, but sometimes vary in their details.

Key ideas: the **Annunciation**. An angel announces to Mary that God will impregnate her and give her a baby who is the son of God. Mary stays a virgin. The **Nativity**: Jesus is born in a manger because King Herod is looking to kill him, because it has been prophesized that he will be king of Jews. Jesus is the son of a carpenter, Joseph and Mary. He is born in Bethlehem. He is visited as a baby by three shepherds, three wise men and three kings. Little is written about his growing up in the Gospels. When he is a young man, John the Baptist begins talking about the coming of the Lord and baptising people to get them ready. He sees Jesus and calls him a "Lamb", the son of God. Jesus goes into the desert and wrestles with the Devil for forty days and nights. He wins and comes back and starts preaching to people about the coming Kingdom of Heaven. He feeds 5000 people with a loaf of bread; he walks on water; he calms the water while on a fishing boat in a storm; he raises Lazarus from the dead. He has twelve disciples, or followers, including Judas and Peter. He communicates his message in "parables": interesting stories with a message. Famous ones are:

The Prodigal Son: there's a good son and a bad son. The bad son spends all the money his Dad has given him on wine, gambling and women. Comes back and has to sleep in father's pig pen to survive. Too ashamed to show his face. His brother finds him and is disgusted. His father sees him and is delighted, announcing there is to be a party about his return and that they should "kill the fatted calf" (the most expensive animal) for the meal.

The house built on sand. There are two houses: one built on firm land. One built on sand. The one on sand is built quickly and looks great. But falls down in a storm. The other one stays up.

The Good Samaritan. A traveller gets beaten up by bandits but is not helped by his fellow men, and instead is rescued from death by a foreigner, a Samaritan.

Jesus gives a "Sermon on the Mount" when he gives a series of famous sayings called the Beatitudes, which are very important and often quoted:

The Beatitudes. Matthew Chapters 5-7 (AKJV): "And seeing the multitudes, he went up into a mountain: and when he was set, his disciples came unto him: and he opened his mouth, and taught them, saying, Blessed are the poor in spirit: for theirs is the kingdom of heaven. 4 Blessed are they that mourn: for they shall be comforted. Blessed are the meek: for they shall inherit the earth. Blessed are they which do hunger and thirst after righteousness: for they shall be filled. Blessed are the merciful: for they shall obtain mercy. Blessed are the pure in heart: for they shall see God. Blessed are the peacemakers: for they shall be called the children of God. Blessed are they which are persecuted for righteousness' sake: for theirs is the kingdom of heaven. Blessed are ye, when men shall revile you, and persecute you, and shall say all manner of evil against you falsely, for my sake."

Jesus is "transfigured". Matthew 17 (AKJV): "And after six days Jesus taketh Peter, James, and John his brother, and bringeth them up into an high mountain apart, 2 and was transfigured before them: and his face did shine as the sun, and his raiment was white as the light. 3 And, behold, there appeared unto them Moses and Elijah talking with him."

Jesus goes into Jerusalem, the holy city, to announce he is the son of God on a donkey (a very lowly animal). He knows he is going to die. He holds a "Last Supper" where bread is broken and wine drunk. He says the bread is his flesh and the wine is his blood. He tells Peter that he will betray him three times before the cock crows.

Betrayal: He is betrayed in the garden of Gethsemane by Judas who kisses him to show the Romans who want to arrest him that he is Jesus. His disciples are asked if they know him. Peter denies knowing him three times before the cock crows.

He is put on trial by Pontius Pilate who washes his hands to indicate he doesn't know what to do with him. The Jewish Pharisees, annoyed by the way Jesus has criticised them, ask for him to be crucify instead one of their men. He is crucified and dies on the Cross. A few days after he is put in his tomb, he is discovered preaching by his disciples. This is the resurrection.

The Ascension: Acts Chapter 1, verses 9-11 (AKJV)
Later, Jesus ascends back to heaven: "And when he had spoken these things, while they beheld, he was taken up; and a cloud received him out of their sight. And while they looked stedfastly

toward heaven as he went up, behold, two men stood by them in white apparel; which also said, Ye men of Galilee, why stand ye gazing up into heaven? this same Jesus, which is taken up from you into heaven, shall so come in like manner as ye have seen him go into heaven. There is a promise though that there will be a "second coming" when Jesus will return to earth to separate the saved and the damned on Judgement Day.

THE REST OF THE NEW TESTAMENT

In Acts, we learn about the story of Paul (formerly Saul) who was a tax collector but on the road to Damascus was converted into believing in Jesus and God. This the story:

Acts 9:1-20 Authorized (AKJV): "And Saul, yet breathing out threatenings and slaughter against the disciples of the Lord, went unto the high priest, and desired of him letters to Damascus to the synagogues, that if he found any of this way, whether they were men or women, he might bring them bound unto Jerusalem. And as he journeyed, he came near Damascus: and suddenly there shined round about him a light from heaven: and he fell to the earth, and heard a voice saying unto him, Saul, Saul, why persecutest thou me? And he said, Who art thou, Lord? And the Lord said, I am Jesus whom thou persecutest: *it is* hard for thee to kick against the pricks. And he trembling and astonished said, Lord, what wilt thou have me to do? And the Lord *said* unto him, Arise, and go into the city, and it shall be told thee what thou must do. And the men which journeyed with him stood speechless, hearing a voice, but seeing no man. And Saul arose from the earth; and when his eyes were opened, he saw no man: but they led him by the hand, and brought *him* into Damascus. And he was three days without sight, and neither did eat nor drink."

He goes on to establish the Christian church but is imprisoned by the Romans for his religious beliefs. In prison, Paul writes a number of letters giving advice to Christians who are setting up the church; Paul invents much the structure of the church.

Book 1 of Corinthians 13, (NIV): This is the most famous lines he wrote: "When I was a child, I talked like a child, I thought like a child, I reasoned like a child. When I became a man, I put the ways of childhood behind me. [12] For now we see only a reflection as in a mirror; then we shall see face to face. Now I know in part; then I shall know fully, even as I am fully known."

The King James Bible**(AKJV)** is much more poetic but more difficult to understand: "When I was a child, I spake as a child, I understood as a child, I thought as a child: but when I became a man, I put away childish things. [12] For now we see through a glass, darkly; but then face to face: now I know in part; but then shall I know even as also I am known. And now abideth faith, hope, charity, these three; but the greatest of these *is* charity."

REVELATIONS

In a nutshell: this is the last book in the New Testament and by far the strangest. Many people have read "occult" signs in it. It tells of the end of the earth and the second coming of Christ, Judgment Day.

Revelation Chapter 6, vs 1-2, New International Version: "I watched as the Lamb opened the first of the seven seals. Then I heard one of the four living creatures say in a voice like thunder, "Come and see!" I looked, and there before me was a white horse! Its rider held a bow, and he was given a crown, and he rode out as a conqueror bent on conquest."

The Lamb is Jesus Christ who opens the book from four horsemen come out: a white horse who symbolises Conquest, a red horse who symbolises War, a black horse who symbolises Famine, and a pale horse who symbolises Death.

Revelation Chapter 6, verses 7-8 (NIV): "When the Lamb opened the fourth seal, I heard the voice of the fourth living creature say, "Come and see!" I looked and there before me was a pale horse! Its rider was named Death, and Hell was following close behind him. They were given power over a fourth of the earth to kill by sword, famine, and plague, and by the wild beasts of the earth."

BABYLON AND THE WHORE OF BABYLON

Basically, a woman, who is a prostitute or harlot, is to blame for the "fallen" state of mankind. **Chapter 17, verse 5 (AKJV)**: "And upon her forehead was a name written a mystery: Babylon The Great, the mother of harlots and abominations of the Earth.... And I saw the woman drunken with the blood of the saints, and with the blood of the martyrs of Jesus: and when I saw her, I wondered with great admiration."

Next step: The Brick Testament is a lot of fun; it's a sort of Lego version of the Bible. Although it's devised for kids, it's a great way of learning the stories. http://thebrickbible.com/

If I am really honest, I have to say that I have found the *The DK Children's Illustrated Bible* (1994) by Selina Hastings the most useful to dip in and out because it presents the stories so attractively and provides some useful contextual points as well. http://www.dk.co.uk/nf/Book/BookDisplay/0,,97814093 64511,00.html

GREEK MYTHS; THE ILIAD AND THE ODYSSEY

Background: Written down in the seventh and eighth century BC, these two long poems remain amongst the most influential stories ever told.

In a nutshell: The Iliad is the story of the ten-year Trojan war and destruction of Troy (Ilium), a great city in the Mediterranean. It tells the story of the battles between the Ancient Greeks (the Achaeans) and the Trojans. Incensed by the theft of his brother's wife, Helen, King Agamemnon sails to Troy with his Greek army to get her back and lays siege to the city of Troy for ten years. Helen has been taken by Paris, the son of King Priam, the Trojan king. Paris was given her as a gift because he judged Aphrodite as the most beautiful of all the goddesses in a beauty contest. The problem was that he had to take her from King Menelaus, Agamemnon's brother, thus triggering a war. Anyway, after many squabbles amongst the Greeks, including a terrible one between Agamemnon and the greatest warrior Achilles, the Greeks win the war by tricking the Trojans to accept the gift of a huge wooden horse. The horse is filled with soldiers who destroy the city when the horse is taken into the centre of Troy. After the war ends, the man who came up with the cunning "wooden horse" plan, Odysseus (sometimes called Ulysses), has great difficulty getting home, getting lost for seven years. His story is called *The Odyssey*; he encounters and defeats the Cyclops (a one-eyed giant), Scylla and Charybdis (two monstrous rocks who smash ships at sea), the Sirens (who sing so sweetly that they lure sailors to their death); he has an affair with the witch-goddess Circe who tries to trap him on her island Calypso forever. Eventually, he gets home only to find that his wife, Penelope and property have been taken over by bands of "suitors" who are all trying to marry Penelope and claim all his belongings. After disguising himself as an old beggar, he defeats the suitors in a bow and arrow contest and they and their serving girls are all killed by him.

There are numerous Greek myths about the Gods and Goddesses, and their interactions with mankind. Overall, they are "capricious": often treating mankind unfairly or with little thought for their well-being. Zeus, the patriarch of the Gods, thinks nothing for example of turning into a swan and raping the beautiful Leda; a story which W.B. Yeats, a modernist Irish poet, writes about in 'Leda and the Swan'.

The Greek drama of Oedipus tells the story of man who unawares kills his father and marries his mother. This story influenced the psycho-analyst Freud when he devised his concept of the "Oedipus Complex": for complicated reasons, Freud believed all men secretly wanted to kill their fathers and marry their mothers. Both the Greek drama and Freud's ideas are very influential.

Influence: Absolutely huge. You'll find references to many of these stories in most literature written before 1950 because so many people were educated by reading these books. James Joyce's 'Ulysses' for example is a very experimental novel which uses the template of 'The Odyssey' as a way of exploring the 'stream of consciousness' thoughts of Leopold Bloom and Stephen Daedalus during one day in Dublin.

Next step: Listen to this BBC programme on 'In Our Time' on *The Odyssey*,
http://www.bbc.co.uk/programmes/p004y297
Read classicist and journalist Charlotte Higgins on *The Iliad*:
http://www.theguardian.com/books/2010/jan/30/iliad-war-charlotte-higgins
Read Lupton & Morden's children versions of the tales, *The Adventures of Achilles* and *The Adventures of Odysseus* (2010). Fantastic re-tellings; they're for children, but adults will learn from them and love them too.
Read Robert Fagles' translations of *The Iliad* (1992, Penguin Classics) and *The Odyssey* (2006, Penguin Classics); they are the most readable and useful.

OLD ENGLISH LITERATURE

In a nutshell: From approximately 600 AD- 1100 AD, there was a rich and fascinating poetic tradition in Britain, some of which was written down, but most of which was spoken. Some fragments from this era survive in written form; they were written in Old English, an Anglo-Saxon dialect, which has some similarities with modern English. Some English courses devote themselves extensively to this time, requiring students to translate Old English in depth. The most famous poem is Beowulf, which tells the story of how the monster Grendel and his monstrous mother terrorise people in their villages and mead halls. Beowulf fights and defeats them both, but is fatally wounded in his last fight. Other poems such as *The Wanderer* talk about the difficult sea-faring life of the people, some recount bloody battles while more religious poems celebrate Christ. The poetry used strong rhythmical lines and is characterized by alliteration.

Next step: Listen to some modern poets, including Seamus Heaney, read modern translations of the poems: http://poemsoutloud.net/columns/archive/the_word_exchange/
Read Seamus Heaney's translation of *Beowulf* (2002, Faber and Faber). This is the best translation you'll find of this seminal poem.

AESOP'S FABLES

In a nutshell: Aesop wrote a number of fables which have entered the collective consciousness of the world. Tales such as *The Hare and the Tortoise*, *The Fox and the Grapes*, *The Wind and the Sun* not only are very familiar children's stories but have also helped shape countless narratives. If you're not that familiar with them, it's worth re-visiting them because you'll see many connections with what you read on any literature course.

Next step: log onto:
http://www.umass.edu/aesop/fables.php
http://www.taleswithmorals.com/

MIDDLE ENGLISH LITERATURE

In a nutshell: After 1066, when William the Conqueror invaded from France, and took over the monarchy in England, literature changes with new French and Latin influences entering into the language of the educated. Geoffrey Chaucer is regarded by many as the originator of English Literature because he wrote *The Canterbury Tales* (1387-1400), a collection of tales told by various pilgrims travelling from Southwark, London to Canterbury Cathedral on a religious pilgrimage. Chaucer's *Prologue* used to be a staple of all English degrees and often A Level courses; here he describes in a comic fashion the pilgrims, painting a picture of a highly religious, hierarchical society, where everyone more or less knows their place. His famous tales include the very chivalrous

The Knight's Tale, the very rude *The Miller's Tale*, the sinister *The Pardoner's Tale* and the energetic *The Wife of Bath's Tale* which is recounted by the Wife of Bath, who is one of the few forceful female characters in the poem.

In the north of England, an anonymous poet wrote Gawain and the Green Knight at about the same time as *The Canterbury Tales*. This poem has more in common with Anglo-Saxon poetry with his use of alliteration and tells the story of Gawain who, in order to win a bet, chops off the head of a knight who is green in colour and then finds, to his alarm, that the knight picks up his head and commands that Gawain must have his head chopped off a year later.

Next step: The University of Glasgow has a useful introduction to the works of Chaucer here:
http://special.lib.gla.ac.uk/exhibns/chaucer/works.html
The BBC has made some lively modern versions of The Canterbury Tales which can be found here:
http://www.bbc.co.uk/drama/canterburytales/
Project Gutenberg has published all of Chaucer online, including audio versions:
http://www.gutenberg.org/browse/authors/c#a144

EARLY MODERN ENGLISH LITERATURE

In a nutshell: The English Reformation, set in train by Henry VIII, when he broke from the Catholic church in 1536, approximately heralds the beginning of the era of 'early modern English': when it was written and spoken. William Tyndale and others undertook the task of translating the Bible into English (it had really only been available in Latin before this) and this arguably led to a great "flourishing" of English Literature, culminating in the golden era of Elizabethan literature which saw the likes of Sir Philip Sidney, Christopher Marlowe and William

Shakespeare publishing poems and plays. Shakespeare wrote most of his works between 1590-1611 when he was living in London and working as an actor. He wrote in early modern English, which is similar to modern English but has a number of significant differences.

Shakespeare wrote numerous plays which were performed in various theatres throughout London. They can be broken down into these "genres": tragedies, comedies, history plays, and the "problem" plays – so called because they are neither . As an English Literature student, you should know:

Tragedies: *Romeo and Juliet, Macbeth, Hamlet, Othello*, King Lear

Comedies: *A Midsummer's Night Dream, 12th Night, Much Ado About Nothing, As You Like It.*

History plays: *Henry IV parts 1 & 2, Henry V, Richard III*

Problem plays: *The Merchant of Venice, The Tempest*

Next step: Read the above plays that you don't know about! Watch them! Look at the movie versions. This website is a good starting point for Shakespeare: http://www.bardweb.net/

You must look at this website to learn more about Shakespeare's language: http://www.shakespeareswords.com/

THE ENLIGHTENMENT

In a nutshell: The Elizabethan period (from 1559-1603) could be termed a "late English Renaissance" because, rather like what happened in Italy over a century before, it marks a huge cultural "re-birth" in the country with the emergence of a national literature, painting and music. From approximately 1650, the scientific philosophy of Francis Bacon and the discoveries of Sir Isaac Newton begin to influence literature as well, as you can see in writer's like John Milton (1608-1674), who attempted to "justify the ways of God to man" by referencing scientific ideas in his epic poem, *Paradise Lost*, which is a "re-write" of the story of the Garden of Eden. Later on, Alexander Pope (1688-1744) would show reverence for both religious and scientific ideas in his witty poetry. Behind much writing of this time is that God is the perfect scientist, shaping and moulding the universe in terms of a perfect order, working much like a watch-maker in knitting together the "clockwork" of nature.

Roughly from 1650 to 1790s, much literature (poems, plays and the first novels) trumpeted the values of the Enlightenment: espousing the triumph of rationality, reason, scientific thinking, and the notion that there was an objective body of 'essential' knowledge that could be learnt. The movement was, in part, used to justify the colonial project because it was developed by colonial powers who claimed that their knowledge was superior to the colonial peoples they were taking over.

Questions to ask of texts in this period: In what way does your text PROMOTE enlightenment values? Does the narrative/text champion rationality, "common sense", and suggest there is "essential" knowledge to be learned?

Next step: Read *Paradise Lost* by John Milton, Books 1 &2, 9&10. I found this website useful; it contains the poem and many links to explanations, videos and books: http://www.paradiselost.org/

THE ROMANTICS

In a nutshell: Reacting against the ideas of the Enlightenment, Romantic poets like William Blake, William Wordsworth, Samuel Coleridge and John Keats wrote poetry which championed the rights of the individual and celebrated the wildness of nature as opposed to its order. They argued that the human imagination, creativity and original thought was more important than scientific methods. They herald the beginnings of what we might recognize as "modernity" in that they expressed feelings of anger and alienation at the emergence of the industrial society. The Romantics valued the imagination and subjectivity above rationality and 'objectivity'; nature was viewed not as the ultimate machine (the Enlightenment view) but as an embodiment of the imagination and the sublime, a concept which suggested awe and wonder.

Questions to ask of texts in this period: In what ways does your text promote Romantic values? Is there a heavy emphasis upon the individual's imagination being more important than the ruling classes' views? Is nature worshipped in the text?

Next step: Read Wordsworth and Coleridge's *Lyrical Ballads*, the seminal text in establishing the Romantic movement. There's an excellent introduction to it here on Radio 4, 'In Our Time':
http://www.bbc.co.uk/programmes/b01cwszf

Read William Blake's *The Songs of Innocence and Experience*:
http://www.blakearchive.org/exist/blake/archive/work.xq?workid=songsie

Read John Keats' poetry:
http://www.poetryfoundation.org/bio/john-keats

THE RISE OF THE NOVEL

In a nutshell: Changes to printing technology and improving literacy meant that substantial numbers of wealthy people could read and enjoyed reading stories. Daniel Defoe (1660-1731) made a successful career as a journalist and wrote what were the forerunners of the modern novel, most famously *Robinson Crusoe* about a man marooned on a desert island, and Molls Flanders which recounts the story of a woman who uses sex as a method of survival and social climbing. Samuel Richardson's *Pamela: Or, Virtue Rewarded* (1740), *Clarissa: Or the History of a Young Lady* (1748) are generally regarded to be the first proper English novels because they explore in depth the emotions of the central characters, using the "epistolary" or letter format. This writing was genuinely "new" – which is what novel or "nouvelle" means in French.

The form was very commercially successful but not regarded by many people as "serious". Most novelists wrote for money not kudos. It was one of the few forms that women were allowed to write in and, as a result, it's perhaps no coincidence that there are many more famous female novelists than there are poets, musicians, and artists. Jane Austen wrote comic novels about romance and class conflict, most notably *Pride and Prejudice* (1813) and *Emma* (1815). Mary Shelley wrote the first science fiction novel, *Frankenstein* (1818). The Bronte sisters invented a new version of the novel which combines elements of the Gothic, romance, social comedy and a Romantic sensibility. Elizabeth Gaskell wrote hard-hitting socially minded novels such as *Mary Barton* (1848), and the first literary biography about Charlotte Bronte, *The Life of Charlotte Bronte* (1857).

The other important novelists of the Victorian period were Charles Dickens (1812-1870), George Eliot (1819-1880) and Thomas Hardy (1840-1828), all of whom were socially minded and used the novel as a way of describing the problems the modern industrial society was facing. From the 1840s until the early 1900s, many writers began espousing views of the Victorian era; there was an emphasis on the form of the novel, which saw its great period of popularity. Writers such as Charles Dickens, George Eliot and Hardy wrote novels which described whole societies. Charlotte Bronte's *Jane Eyre* (1847) is very Victorian in its sensibility; there is a sense of narrative coherence, its endorsement of patriarchal values and an embracing of a social panorama in the text. In many ways, Andrea Levy's modern novel *Small Island* (2004) embraces many aspects of the Victorian novel in the way it attempts to offer a social realist perspective and embrace a social panorama; there is a neatness about the narrative which is typically always "wrapped" up with a neatly structured, "closed" ending.

Questions to ask of texts in this period: Does your text try encompass the whole of society? Does it have an omniscient third person narrator who appears to know everything? Is there a coherent, "neatly tied up" narrative?

Next step: Read Austen's *Pride and Prejudice*, Shelley's *Frankenstein*, Dickens' *Great Expectations* and Thomas Hardy's *Tess of the D'Urbervilles*.

LITERARY MOVEMENTS: MODERNISM

In a nutshell: After the First World War, many writers and artists experimented with the 'form' of the novel, dispensing with things like traditional narratives or 'coherent' characters. Their great theme was the alienation of modern man from his society. T.S. Eliot's *The Wasteland*, James Joyce's *Ulysses*, and Kafka's *The Trial* were all part of this. Some writers straddle the periods of modernism and post-modernism such as Jean Rhys who wrote a number of modernist novels during the 1920s and 30s, and then published *Wide Sargasso Sea* in the 1960s, a text which shares both modernist and post-modernist tropes.

Questions to ask of texts in this period: Does your text experiment with form quite self-consciously? Does the text appear fragmented and deliberately incomplete? Are there many allusions to other texts? Does a deep-rooted sense of alienation permeate the text?

Next step: Read T.S. Eliot's *The Wasteland*, Kafka's *Metamorphosis*, James Joyce's *Portrait of the Artist as a Young Man* and Virginia Woolf's *To The Lighthouse*.

LITERARY MOVEMENT: POST-MODERNISM

In a nutshell: From the 1960s-present day, post-modernists work in many different art forms from novels to architecture. They believe in "quoting" from the past in a playful fashion; the Canary Wharf tower is typically "post-modern" with its references to tower blocks and the Egyptian pyramids. Many post-modern texts are self-consciously "inter-textual"; they reference other texts, enter into conversations with them. *Wide Sargasso Sea* is post-modern in the way it engages with a dialogue with *Jane Eyre*.

Questions to ask about texts of this period: When was your text written? Does it play with form and reference many other "periods" of art?

Next step: Read Jean Rhys's *Wide Sargasso Sea*, Angela Carter's *Nights at the Circus* and Salman Rushdie's *Midnight's Children.*

HISTORICAL CONCEPT: COLONIALISM

In a nutshell: Many texts written in English between 1750-1960 embrace colonial values in that they endorse either explicitly or indirectly the colonial project; these texts (such as James Bond/Agatha Christie/much 'nationalist' poetry) typically offer the view that white European people are far superior than their colonial subjects.

Questions to ask of texts of this period: What kind of colonial discourses are embedded within the text? Are there racist views in the text, or views of other cultures which are very stereotypical?

Next step: Read *The Penguin Book of Caribbean Verse*, Rudyard Kipling's *Kim.*

HISTORICAL CONCEPT: POST-COLONIALISM

In a nutshell: Post-colonial texts, such as *Wide Sargasso Sea*, *The Kite Runner*, much Caribbean poetry, and *Small Island*, critique the colonial project, promoting more egalitarian views of colonised subjects.

Questions to ask of these texts: Does the text explore the social injustices of the colonial project? Does the text examine, investigate, represent the subaltern in a meaningful and complex fashion? Does the text give a chance for oppressed minorities to speak?

Next step: Read *The Penguin Book of Caribbean Verse*.
Watch this excellent series of Yale lectures on YouTube on structuralism, post-structuralism and literary theory:
http://www.youtube.com/playlist?list=PL5F8BF9823576D9DB

SPELLING, PUNCTUATION AND GRAMMAR YOU REALLY MUST KNOW ABOUT

A surprising number of English graduates are shaky on certain areas connected with spelling, punctuation and grammar. This may be because they've always got by without really knowing how language works; they have spent their time reading literature and writing essays, rather than doing grammatical analysis. I got a good English degree without knowing about the apostrophe rule for "its" and "it's"!

Grammar is a very tricky area. First, it's difficult to define what it is, although the term is used very widely in connection with English. Second, if you're an English graduate and you're not that confident about talking about "grammar" you can find yourself being mocked by the outside world! In this section, I've defined grammar as being the "meta-language" or "terminology" we use to talk about the mechanics of language.

GRAMMAR – WORD CLASSES

Nouns. There are two major types of nouns: concrete nouns and abstract nouns. Concrete nouns are tangible objects/things/people/places that can be touched, felt, and seen: door, chair, person, London. Abstract nouns are concepts or ideas such as faith, hope, charity. Concrete nouns bring the world into being. In a piece of writing, they are used to create a sense of a world; through the deployment of nouns we learn about the people, the places and the things are central to the story or poem. It is extremely useful to look at the different nouns being used in a passage to get a sense as to how a writer is creating a sense of a world.

Pronouns. Pronouns take the place of a noun and are extremely important in texts because they tell you about the "person" a text is written in; whether it is "first person" and written using "I" or "We" as the narrator or "third person", whether it is told from the perspective or "he/she or they". This has a profound effect upon the tone, attitude and approach of a text.

Verbs. These are "doing" words. The grammar of verbs can be complicated, but if we were being really simple, you could argue that there are two main types of verbs: dynamic and stative. Dynamic verbs create a sense of action, such as "to say", "jumped", "kicked". They create a sense of movement, of action in a text. Stative verbs are much less dynamic such as the verb "to be" and "to have": they are not dynamic and usually state what "is" the case, e.g. "The man is here", "I have the money".

Adjectives. Adjectives describe nouns. They bring colour and emotion to a text, e.g. the beautiful sky, the angry person.

Adverbs. Adverbs are used to modify a verb, adjective or another adverb, e.g. Mo writes *beautifully*; Jim cries *profusely*. Like adjectives they often can help create the mood or atmosphere of a text and are worth looking at from this point of view.

Next step. For more on word classes please log onto: http://www.ucl.ac.uk/internet-grammar/ This website is specifically geared towards university undergraduates and covers all the basics and then some more.

BBC Skillswise is also very useful: http://www.bbc.co.uk/skillswise/english

SPELLING

Obviously it is vital to spell correctly in your work. The most common error I see is the incorrect use of homophones: words that sound the same but are spelt differently. The worst mistakes I've seen are: "there, their, and they're". For more on this please log onto:

https://owl.english.purdue.edu/engagement/index.php?category_id=2&sub_category_id=1&article_id=48

PUNCTUATION

The biggest thing I've noticed graduates could learn about is the correct use of the comma, semi-colon and colon. The English department at UCL have an excellent website that covers all the main areas:

http://www.ucl.ac.uk/english/Punctuation_guide

ESSAY WRITING

CASE STUDY: ANN, THE PROCRASTINATOR

Ann was really good about her reading and note-taking. This was the thing she really loved about her English course: sitting down in the library and reading, browsing, sifting through books of all shapes and sizes. However, the one thing she was really bad at was actually sitting down to write an essay. She'd always read a great deal before writing an essay, and usually wouldn't actually sit down to write anything until a day before the essay was due. As a result, her essays were always rushed, usually quite poorly structured and often handed in late. She always told herself that she wasn't going to do things this way, that next time, she'd do the reading sooner and then write the essay maybe a week before it was due. But every time she broke her rule because she became so immersed in her reading.

What should Ann do?

I would strongly recommend she starts writing as soon as she can and NOT worry about having done all the reading. She should read the text which is the main topic for discussion, then write a rough draft with her thoughts on it. And then, if she has time, do some extra reading. That way, she can integrate her own thoughts with other people's. A repeated idea that I've said in this guide is that WE THINK THROUGH WRITING! You'll find that as you write about a topic, new thoughts will come to you. Now, it may be that you discard or amend those thoughts as you write more or read more, but at least you'll be "on your way" with some ideas. It's better to write early and often, than late and in a rushed fashion.

The next thing is Ann should ask for some guidance from her tutors. One student told me: "It was very difficult to write essays for university initially: I did not realise the significant difference in writing between A Level and university. Support from tutorials was exceptional however, and would still find difficulty if not for their help."

One of the most troubling and stressful issues for students at university is essay writing. There are a number of reasons for this. First, there is usually a lot riding on essay writing. Quite a bit of the time, they are formally assessed and the mark contributes towards your final degree; in this sense, they are "high stakes" pieces of writing. If you don't get them right, your prospects could suffer. Secondly, many students feel particularly bad if they don't get good marks; they feel worthless. Most undergraduates' sense of self, their self-worth, can be severely dented if they feel they are not good at writing essays.

There are three simple pieces of advice if you want to get good marks with your essay writing:

Practice, practice, practice. Write rough drafts and re-draft your work. Give yourself plenty of time. Don't be afraid just to get down to writing bits of your essay early on and then don't be afraid to chuck it all away.

Read, read, read. The wider your reading of other essays, both published and unpublished ones, the better you'll get. You'll get a feel for the different types of essay.

Discuss, discuss, discuss. The more you talk about the issues that you are writing about, the better you'll get at formulating a decent argument. Discuss your essay with your tutors; make an appointment to see them, tell them your ideas, listen and take notes on what they have to say. Discuss the issues with your fellow students: form a book group, a small discussion group. Talk about the key themes in the pub, in the coffee shop, in the street. **Bearing these major points in mind, let's look at a few other things as well.**

TAKE OWNERSHIP OF THE QUESTION

"The way essay questions are worded is very annoying. When the question does not make technical, grammatical sense it is very difficult to reply to. Deciphering the question was usually the thing I needed help with." English Literature student

This is vital. Most English departments are very helpful because they issue many of the questions at the very beginning of the course and publish them on their Virtual Learning Environments. Look at them now! Write down the questions when you go to a lecture, take notes bearing in mind the particular essay question, think and mull over the question in your mind, jotting down thoughts that come to you.

Make the question *your* question. Tease over the phrases of the question in your mind and think about what you can bring to the question. Many good essays "problematize" a question; that is, they unpick the assumptions behind a question and use that to analyse the selected texts. They use the question as a way of entering into a dialogue or conversation with a text. The Russian theorist Mikhail Bakhtin proposed in his seminal book, *The Dialogic Imagination* that a reader constructs the meanings of a text by entering into a dialogue with it in their mind. Often, essay questions help you enter into this dialogue; they give you a focus, a beam of light to shine upon the words in a text.

STAGES IN WRITING ESSAYS

I'm going to propose that you use the acronym BOL to help you write your essays. That is:

Brainstorm

Order

Link

The brainstorming phase is the FIRST THING you do. If you've got coursework, start BRAINSTORMING as soon as you can; this means getting all your thoughts, quotations, points together in a notebook or on the computer in one document. Rule NOTHING OUT at this stage. This is the place where you give yourself FREEDOM to think the unthinkable. Switch off the internal critic who tells you that your ideas are rubbish, and GO FOR IT! This is just as important in an exam as it is when you doing coursework and have got weeks to think about a question. It's very important to give yourself intellectual room; this relaxes you and gives you the chance to really explore areas of interest. As a general rule, follow your interests and passions; better to write a bad passionate essay than a lifeless so-called good one. Tutors at University want to be gripped and engaged, they don't want tepid, second-hand ideas.

Once you've got your notes together, you need to read through them carefully and ORDER them. That is, arrange them in some kind of meaningful fashion. While you're doing this, you should be making LINKS or connections between your points so that your essay reads smoothly. It is strongly recommended at this stage that you discuss your essay with someone. A good technique is to present your essay to another student, explaining in clear English what your argument is in RESPONSE to the question. Equally, you could discuss the issue with the relevant tutor. There's a great deal of evidence to suggest that if students talk through their notes before writing it, then things become clearer in their minds.

THE PROCESS OF WRITING ESSAYS

Here are some quotes from various English Literature students that you may find helpful:

> "There is less of a 'tick box' approach and more focus on quality, but it is still unclear what this is and what we are marked on."

> "Do the essays as soon as you get them."

> "I feel fairly confident about essay writing, but I've found my tutors helpful for extra advice/help."

> "Fairly confident but more support from seminar tutors would be nice – all my essays felt like a shot-in-the-dark slightly."

"Needed some help with sentence structure, went to EAW, they were really helpful. Some tutors held feedback sessions and some not. Feel more confident in coursework essays, though in exams out seminar tutor didn't touch upon exam prep at all really."

"The exam is completely stupid and archaic, look to universities in Scandinavia and set up technological facilities for us to produce work that is actually comparable to what we have been doing for our coursework."

"Not very confident – felt very guided at A Level, we were given specific ways in which to respond. Whereas at uni, it feels like it's a bit of a free-flow just go with it. Often I'm not sure if I'm doing it right or not."

THE DIFFERENT TYPES OF ESSAYS

There are two major intellectual processes that usually go on in most essays: **deductive** and **inductive** reasoning.

Deductive reasoning starts with making general points, formulating a generalised argument and then looking at the particular. For example, if you were writing an essay on *Othello*, you might make a statement such as "Jealousy can be very destructive" and then examine the ways in which Othello's jealousy leads to him killing his wife, Desdemona, because he suspects her of having an affair with another man. If you were taking an inductive approach, you'd be taking the opposite approach; you'd look at the evidence in the play, and then show that Othello's jealousy is destructive. Induction starts with the particular and then generalises having examined it. **Inductive reasoning** moves from the particular to the general.

Your essays will shift between the two approaches, but it is important to understand that they are quite different ways of reasoning because they both have strengths and weaknesses. The deductive approach can risk not finding sufficient evidence to back up its central argument, while the inductive approach can get lost in the "particulars" of a text and then never formulate any generalised points. English Literature students regularly fall into both traps: some students make too many generalised arguments without any evidence to back them up, while others are so bogged down in analysing a text that they never quite offer an overview.

Introductions. Hmmnn. Personally, I have some big concerns about some students' introductions. Too often they read more like unproven conclusions; bold statements about the question which never are substantiated. Other introductions are very clunky and expose the student's thought processes too explicitly by listing everything they are going to do in an essay. This isn't really that necessary. There are no set ways of writing an introduction, but if I were to make a recommendation it would be to leave your introduction to last when drafting. It's often beneficial in your first rough drafts to get stuck in right away and start with a quotation or a statement that you substantiate with evidence. Begin in "media res" – in the middle of things.

The main body of an essay. This is the meat of the essay and will need to be carefully structured. Again, with the undergraduate essay there are no set ways of structuring your essay, but there are some well-worn approaches which are worth considering.

THE DIALECTICAL ESSAY.

This is an essay which deals with thesis (argument) and antithesis (counter-argument), which leads to synthesis (a point which synthesises the essence of the argument and the counter-argument).

Let's imagine for a moment that the essay title is: "Examine the representation of jealousy in *Othello.*"

In order to write this type of essay, it is useful to plan in this way:

Arguments for: Othello is represented primarily as a jealous husband (FIND EVIDENCE FOR THIS POINT)

Arguments against: Othello's jealousy is secondary compared to his obsession with loss of status (FIND EVIDENCE FOR THIS POINT)

Synthesis: Othello's jealousy is fuelled by his insecurity over his position in Venetian society; Shakespeare paints a picture of a society which fundamentally views Othello as the "Other".

The "dialectical" essay is excellent at dealing with different viewpoints. Problems can occur when student veer away from the question which can happen if you're not vigilant.

THE EVIDENCE-BASED ESSAY: USING THE 5WS + H.

This is primarily an "inductive" essay in that most of the points are shaped around textual evidence. Typically, this kind of essay will move from point to point by examining quotation from the primary texts. This kind of essay will use the 5Ws + H to help analyse the textual evidence:

What? What is happening in the quotation?

Who? Who is speaking? Who is writing the text? Who is the text aimed at?

Where? Where is the text set? Where was the text written? Where is the text going?

When? When was the text written? When does this moment happen in the text?

Why? For all the above questions, you need to ask the question: why is this important to consider? Why are we reading this text?

How? How is the text creating its effects?

This kind of essay is often structured around the concept of "PEEing"! You may well have been taught this to death at school:

Point: Othello's jealousy is represented as deeply destructive.

Evidence: Killing of Desdemona, His suicide

Explanation/Analysis: Analyse relevant quotation from these two scenes using 5Ws + H

This approach is entirely valid but it can be very "programmatic" and many essays written in this style can come across as written by robots! I'm all for "PEEing" when it's appropriate, but if you do it too much, the essay can become stilted. Undergraduate essays are marked for their style and finesse as well as for their ability to produce valid evidence and analysis; PEEing too much can lead to a very dry essay. This said, it is entirely valid technique when used APPROPRIATELY.

THE THEMED ESSAY.

This kind of essay groups the key points to be addressed in a question around key themes. So, for example, with the *Othello* essay, a themed approach might look at the different types and stages of jealousy represented in the play.

Theme 1: Othello's jealousy
Theme 2: Iago's jealousy of Othello
Theme 3: The destructive effects of Othello and Iago's jealousy

THE CRITICAL PERSPECTIVES ESSAY.

This is a style of essay that you've possibly not done before but which focuses upon either one or more than one critical approach to a text.

For example, the *Othello* question could be approached by examining different theoretical approaches towards the representation of jealousy. I have suggested possible approaches briefly here, but if you are interested in following up on any of them, look up the page numbers provided here from Pope (2012) and they will give you a more in-depth guide to deploying these critical approaches.

Critical perspective 1
A feminist interpretation of the representation of jealousy, looking at the ways in which patriarchal discourses permeate the language of Othello and Iago, objectifying women as possessions and sexual objects. (Pope, 163-74)

Critical perspective 2
A Marxist interpretation of the representation of jealousy. Both men are the victims of a rigid class structure in which their

positions are insecure, their jealousy is a manifestation of this insecurity. (Pope, 155-63)

Critical perspective 3

A psycho-analytical interpretation. Both Othello and Iago are repressed homosexuals who's jealousy is a manifestation of their latent desire for each other. (Pope, 147-50)

Critical perspective 4

A post-colonial interpretation. Othello's jealousy is linked to his troubled identity as both an imperialist commander and a black man. (Pope, pp. 183-97)

Do you see how all four of these interpretations could lead to richly suggestive and interesting essays? The advantage of this approach is that it does yield "high level" deductive and inductive reasoning. The disadvantage can be that there is TOO much for one essay. It may be that just taking a close look at one approach might be more productive than covering all the approaches mentioned in the chart.

CONCLUSIONS

What is the point of a conclusion? The object of a conclusion is to "sum up" or crystallise the main points of your essay. You should be making THREE or FOUR points in a conclusion to a 1,500 word essay that sums up the key points of your essay. Perhaps more if your essay is longer. This doesn't mean you REPEAT points you have already made, it means that you BRING TOGETHER or synthesize your key points into a FINDING. This is not the same thing as making a new point; the evidence for your conclusions should have been discussed in your essay. Crucially, you should check that you haven't actually written your conclusion in your introduction, where you've made summative comments about what you've found when analysing the relevant texts.

Next step: Reading University has produced a very helpful, detailed booklet, which can be downloaded as PDF, about using the correct style in essays:

http://blogs.reading.ac.uk/engage-in-teaching-and-learning/files/2012/10/Style-Guide-for-English-Literature-students.pdf

Warwick University has provided a good explanation about how to write an English literature essay on the web. Although it is aimed at a specific module on seventeenth century literature, I thought it was of general use:

http://www2.warwick.ac.uk/fac/arts/english/currentstudents/undergraduate/modules/fulllist/second/en228/how_to_write_an_essay/

ANALYSING LANGUAGE

The following exercises are devised by me but based on my reading of an extremely useful book: *Reading poetry : an introduction* by Furniss and Bath.

FIGURATIVE LANGUAGE – THE ACID TEST

Figurative Language is a general term for a group of linguistic devices called figures of speech (p. 146, Furniss).

A word, phrase or statement is figurative when it cannot be taken literally in the context in which it is being used, for example: "love is blind", "look before you leap" = could be literal and figurative.

Figurative or not?

The light at the end of the tunnel…

The glass half full

Well, it all depends upon the context. If you are really in a tunnel and you can see a light in front of you, then it's not figurative at all but literal, but if you are struggling with a problem and you begin to see how to solve it, you may say a phrase like there's light at the end of the tunnel, making your language figurative. The same applies with "the glass half full"; you could literally be looking at a glass half full of water, or talking about your situation in life and figuratively describing it that way.

METONYMY AND SYNECDOCHE

Metonymy means 'change of name'; it is a figure of speech in which the name of one thing is used to name something which is associated with it – as in 'the pen is mightier than the sword'. Not literally true. 'Pen' means 'writing or writers'.

E.g. 'The White House denied rumours' = the WH represents the government

A figure which is related to metonymy is 'synecdoche'. Synecdoche works mainly through two associative principles: 'part of the whole' and 'container for contained'. Eg 'All hands on decks' does not literally mean chopped off hands to be on deck, it means the sailors etc...

"Metaphor *creates* the relation between its objects, while **metonymy** *presupposes* that relation."
(Hugh Bredin, "Metonymy." *Poetics Today*, 1984)

Examples

"The suits on Wall Street walked off with most of our savings."

Wall Street = metonymy because it stands in for stockbrokers and bankers

"Lend me your ears..."

Ears = synecdoche because one small object (ears) stands in for a bigger whole (your body)

"He loves the bottle"

Bottle = metonymy because the bottle represents alcohol.

"He is loyal to the crown"

Crown = synecdoche because one small object represents the whole of the monarchy.

METAPHOR

Metaphor is quite simply when one thing is compared to another without any "like" or "as" in between: "the sun has got his hat on"; "the boxer was a bear"; "his anger was volcanic". It works on the assumption that there are similarities between things. Used in all kinds of language.

All discourses have their own characteristic metaphors.

ANALYSIS OF METAPHOR

Tenor = what is being talked about
Vehicle = the metaphorical way it's being talked about
Ground = the similarities between tenor and vehicle/connotations of the metaphor
E.g. "An Englishman's home is his castle"
Tenor (what is being talked about) = "an Englishman's home"
Vehicle (metaphorical term) = "his castle"
Ground = the similarities between the tenor and vehicle (eg Englishman is lord and master, safe in his home)
Work out these ones:
The classroom was a bearpit
The cesspit of humanity
Answers
The classroom was a bear pit
Tenor = classroom
Vehicle = bear pit
Ground = the classroom is being personified as a wild animal, connoting ill-discipline, poor behavior etc
The cesspit of humanity
Tenor = humanity
Vehicle = cesspit
Ground = suggesting that people, humans, are like a sewer, dirty, corrupt etc.

DEAD METAPHOR AND POETIC METAPHOR

Shelley in *A Defence of Poetry* (1821): "Poetry lifts the veil from the hidden beauty of the world, makes familiar objects be as if they were not familiar". This is very similar to the Russian Formalists' concept of "defamiliarisation".

Defamiliarization is an artistic technique, used in poetry and novels, to force the reader to see an ordinary situation in an entirely different way. For example, Kafka "defamiliarized" the way we see officials and bureaucracy in novels like The Trial by telling the story of a man, K, who is arrested but never told why he is arrested, and instead spends most of his time being passed from one official to another. Science Fiction often defamiliarises ordinary situations by setting them in a different context. Some critics have argued that Orwell's *1984* is really about the privations of post-war Europe rather being the science fiction novel it purports to be.

Look at these lines and say whether you can work out:
The tenor
The vehicle
The ground
Whether the image is "dead" or "poetic"
"Shall I compare thee to a summer's day?"
"You are the light in my life!"

Answers

You could argue that both images are "dead" because although Shakespeare's famous opening line to his sonnet "Shall I compare thee to a summer's day" was once original, it is now so commonly said that it has lost its power. It once was poetic but is no longer. The other phrase, "You are the light of my life!" is a cliché and too familiar to be treated as poetic.

POETIC SYMBOL

The New Princeton Encyclopedia of Poetry and Poetics (1993) says that poetic symbol is "a kind of figurative language in which what is shown (normally referring to something material) means, by virtue of some sort of resemblance, suggestion or association, something more or something else (normally immaterial)". There is a specific tenor but it is not certain what the "vehicle" is, there is no specific reference.

There is a specific tenor but it is not certain what the 'vehicle' is, there is no specific reference.

The Symbolist movement focused upon the suggestive power of Symbols

Look at this poem by William Blake and how and why it is a symbolic poem:

> O Rose thou art sick.
> The invisible worm,
> That flies in the night
> In the howling storm:
>
> Has found out thy bed
> Of crimson joy:
> And his dark secret love
> Does thy life destroy.

This poem has been much written about because ultimately we don't know what the "tenor" – what is being talked about – actually is. Clearly, the "Rose" is not a real rose, it is a "vehicle" of some sort but the tenor is never fully explained. As a result, we can only speculate about possible "tenors" and this can lead to some rich, complex and speculative criticism. The specific 'tenor' is missing and as a result makes the poem symbolic.

RHYTHM

Definitions

Prosody = the study of rhythm in poetry, sometimes called metrical analysis.

Rhythm is the BEAT of language: it is the most important element of language when combined with meaning. You could say that rhythm is the heart-beat of language.

In order to "get" the rhythm of a poem you should:

1. Read the poem out aloud.

2. Then clap out the rhythm.

3. Then think about the effects of the rhythm: what does it make you think, feel and see? What is the difference between rhythm and rhyme?

Rhythm = the beat of the poem, where the hard and soft stresses go.

Rhyme = is where there are similar sounds, usually vowel sounds, that chime together, eg blue shoe poo you

The most important thing with rhythm and rhyme is to discuss the **effects** they create: what mood does the rhythm create? What ideas/themes/images/emotions does it emphasize or highlight?

There are two major types of rhythm: rising rhythm and falling rhythm.

Rising rhythm is created by two major types of "stress patterns" or metrical feet: iambs and anapaests. An iamb is a metrical feet which consists of a soft beat followed by a hard one: di-DUM. It is the most common kind of rhythm found in poetry and speech. If we go back to the opening line of Shakespeare's famous sonnet we can see how the line is iambic, when read aloud you can hear how the stresses fall where I have marked the syllables in bold:

Shall **I** com**pare** thee **to** a **sum**mer's **day**?

The other type of rising rhythm is the anapaest which consists of two soft stresses followed by a hard stress: di-di-DUM. One of William Blake's most rhythmically joyous poems is called *Laughing Song* from *the Songs of Innocence*. This poem really works when you read it aloud and clap the rhythm: it is genuinely like a song; you can just imagine a drum beat making the poem come alive. The poem is largely "anapaestic"; that is, it is full of fast-paced metrical feet called anapaests which create a fantastically energetic tone; the rhythm is always "rising". Let's look at the first verse, the heavy beats are in bold:

When the **green** woods **laugh** with the **voice** of **joy** (anapest, iamb, anapest, iamb)
And the **dimp**ling **stream** runs **laugh**ing **by**, (anapest, iamb,

iamb, iamb)
When the **air** does **laugh** with our **mer**ry **wit**, (anapest, iamb, anapest, iamb)
And the **green** hill **laughs** with the **noise** of **it**. (anapest, iamb, anapest, iamb)

Falling rhythm. The other type of rhythm is the falling rhythm which creates often the sensation of "falling" because the hard stress comes first and is followed by a soft stress. A trochee consists of a hard beat followed by a soft one: DUM-di. William Blake's *The Lamb* is a classic example of this:

> **Litt**le **Lamb** who **made** thee
> **Dost** thou **know** who **made** thee
> **Gave** thee **life** & **bid** thee feed,
> **By** the **stream** & **o'er** the mead;
> **Gave** thee **cloth**ing of de**light**,
> **Soft**est **cloth**ing **wooly bright**;
> **Gave** thee **such** a **tend**er **voice**,
> **Mak**ing **all** the **vales** re**joice**:
> **Litt**le **Lamb** who **made** thee
> **Dost** thou **know** who **made** thee

The other type of "falling" rhythm is the dactyl which consists of a hard beat followed by two soft ones: DUM-di-di. It is not a common metre but you can see a "falling" dactylic rhythm emerging in some poems. William Blake's Holy Thursday from the *Songs of Innocence* shows a dactylic rhythm in places but it also exemplifies some of the problems which can happen with metrical analysis. Let's look at the first verse:

> **Twas** on a **Ho**ly **Thurs**day their **inn**ocent **fac**es **clean**
> The **chil**dren **walk**ing **two** & **two** in **red** & **blue** & **green**
> **Grey** headed **bead**les **walk**d before with **wands** as **white** as **snow**
> **Till** into the **high** dome of **Pauls** they like **Thames** waters **flow**

If you look at the first line, you can see that it begins with a dactyl (**Twas** on a) followed by a trochee (**Holy**) but then a strange thing happens in the line, there is, if you read it carefully, a distinct pause or what is known as a "caesura" – a break in the line – and the rhythm becomes a rising one after this: there's an iamb followed by an anapest and an iamb:

"their **inn**ocent **fac**es **clean**" (iamb, anapest, iamb)

This line shows the problems with metrical analysis; if you're not careful you can really get tied up into knots! But this said, you can use it to analyse poetry in an interesting way because if you look back at that opening line of Blake's you can see that the poet has a falling rhythm on his announcement of the day of "Holy Thursday", but a rising rhythm when describing the children; you could argue there's a mournful rhythm on his proclamation of the day, but a positive one when describing the children, which exactly chimes with the message of the poem which appears to argue that it is the human spirit and not human rituals which create meaning in life.

Use these descriptions to help you describe the effect of the rhythm:

Fast: speedy; fast-paced; quick; lively; energetic; enthusiastic; passionate; fiery;

Slow; sluggish; heavy; slow-paced; emphatic; leaden; lethargic; tired; lugubrious; gloomy;

Next step: read Furniss and Bath, *Reading Poetry*, chapter 12.

USING ACRONYMS TO PROMPT THOUGHTS

A good way of making sure that you are detailed in your analysis of language is to devise your own acronym to help you cover the points that your course expects you to. This is one possible acronym:

FREE 5 TIGERS

Each letter represent a type of analysis:

Figure it out -- use your intuition, always THINK!

Rhyme – look for the way a poem rhymes and why it rhymes that way.

Evidence -- everything has to be backed up with evidence/quotation.

Explanation – explain what is happening in a quote.

5 Ws – e.g. What is happening? Where is it happening? Who is it happening to? When did it happen? Why is it being written about?

Themes – Discuss the ideas and concept that are explored in a text

Imagery – Look at all the poetic devices in a text: the metaphors, similes, personification, onomatopoeia, alliteration

Genre – Look at the type of text, and the conventions of that genre; how does the text both conform and subvert the genre?

Evaluation – How effective is the text and why?

Rhythm – Analyse the rhythmic effects in the language.

Structure – Analyse the structure of the text and think about how its form and structure shape meanings in a text.

Think of your own acronym to help you analyse the poems.

Next step: This crib sheet from the University of Texas is useful: http://uwc.utexas.edu/handouts/poetry-analysis/
Read *Reading Poetry* by Furniss and Bath!

REMEMBER YOU ARE NOT ALONE

I'm giving the last word to students themselves:

> "Essay marking seemed very arbitrary. My marks never corresponded to the quality of the writing. I'm not sure what criteria was used."

> "Advice: talk to your tutors."

> "Often I feel that everyone else is more in tune with what is wanted and has a more insightful or artistic view on a text.

This, at times, leaves me feeling inadequate and unsure of my capabilities."

"I found it difficult obtaining secondary reading. I was always unsure of what to read and spent a lot of time looking at irrelevant areas. The tutors were mostly very helpful however."

"I have really struggled with my confidence, but eventually spoke to the disability team/seminar tutor who really helped me, I would advise students who are anxious to seek help as fast as possible."

"BE PROVOCATIVE, BE ORGANISED."

"Having a job (I get a minimum loan, but I don't want to take any money off my parents) meant that even brilliant organisation wouldn't make all the reading possible. This year felt like more a year of finding the motivation to study in the face of all kinds of problems: applied too late for halls, house is falling apart, fell out with a housemate, we're getting evicted. I'm very depressed, various incidents, leaks, no water, theft by strange men. I have mates who bring perverts home, and life generally feels like a soap opera."

"I hope to gain a wider understanding of human creativity, pop culture and literary history so I can reference this in my own work. Poetic language is a good start. I wish I'd read more this year, a new student should get ahead and read. You need to motivate yourself; smoking weed gets in the way."

SELECT BIBLIOGRAPHY

Baker, J. & Myszor, F. (2000) *Living Literature – Exploring Advanced Level Literature.* UK. Hodder and Stoughton.

Bloom, H. (1997) *The Anxiety of Influence: A Theory of Poetry.* USA. OUP.

Castle, G. (2013) *The Literary Theory Handbook (Blackwell Literature Handbooks)* UK. Wiley-Blackwell.

Eagleton, T. (1996a) *Literary Theory – An Introduction.* UK. Wiley-Blackwell.

Eagleton, T. (1996b) "Phenomenology, Hermeneutics, and Reception Theory," in *Literary Theory.* USA. University of Minnesota Press, p. 47 – 78.

Furniss, T. & Bath, M. (2007) *Reading poetry : an introduction,* Harlow, Pearson Longman.

Glendinning, S. (2011) *Derrida – A Very Short Introduction.* UK. Oxford University Press.

Larkin, P. (2012) *The Complete Poems.* UK. Faber and Faber.

Singer, P. (1980) *Marx – A Very Short Introduction.* OUP

Snapper, G. (2009), *Beyond English Literature A Level: The silence of the seminar?.* English in Education, 43: 192–210.

Shakespeare, W. (2001) *Othello – Arden Shakespeare. Third Series.* Arden Shakespeare.

Young, T. (2008) *Studying English Literature – A Practical Guide.* Cambridge University Press.

ABOUT THE AUTHOR

Francis Gilbert is a writer who has been a secondary school teacher for over twenty years in various London schools. He has published numerous books, including *I'm A Teacher, Get Me Out Of Here* and *The Last Day of Term* as well as a series of study guides on classic texts such *Frankenstein*, *Wuthering Heights* and *Jane Eyre* -- all published on Kindle. He currently lectures in English at a university and teaches part-time in a large comprehensive. He is completing a PhD in Creative Writing and Education for which he is writing an autobiographically-inspired novel, *Who Do You Love?*. He is particularly interested in the ways in which teachers can cultivate a sense of beauty in their students by using the tools of the internet. You can learn more about his work by logging onto his website: www.francisgilbert.co.uk

Printed in Poland
by Amazon Fulfillment
Poland Sp. z o.o., Wrocław